Successful Christian Parenting

Nurturing with Insight
and Disciplining in Love

Doug Britton
Marriage and Family Counselor

BibleSource Publications
Sacramento, California

ISBN 1-930153-11-2

PD20030210

Printed in the United States of America

BibleSource Publications
Sacramento CA
www.biblesource.net

Now to him who is able to do immeasurably more than all we ask or imagine, according to his power that is at work within us, to him be glory in the church and in Christ Jesus throughout all generations, for ever and ever! Amen (Ephesians 3:20-21).

BOOKS BY DOUG BRITTON

Conquering Depression: A Journey Out of Darkness into God's Light
Defeating Temptation: Biblical Secrets to Self-Control
Healing Life's Hurts: God's Solutions When Others Wound You
Overcoming Jealousy and Insecurity: Biblical Steps to Living without
  Fear
Self-Concept: Understanding Who You are in Christ
Strengthening Your Marriage: 12 Exercises for Married Couples
Successful Christian Parenting: Nurturing with Insight and
  Disciplining in Love
Victory Over Grumpiness, Irritation and Anger

Marriage by the Book (eight-book series)
1: Laying a Solid Foundation
2: Making Christ the Cornerstone
3: Encouraging Your Spouse
4: Extending Grace to Your Mate
5: Talking with Respect and Love
6: Improving Your Teamwork
7: Putting Money in its Place
8: Fanning the Flames of Romance
Marriage by the Book Group Leaders' Guide

Visit www.DougBrittonBooks.com to see a current list
of all books by Doug Britton

Contents

Preface   7

Introduction   9

PART I: CREATE A NURTURING HOME

1   *Communicate with Respect and Love*   21

2   *Center Your Home in the Lord*   39

3   *Care for Yourself and Your Marriage*   62

PART II: EXERCISE AUTHORITY (GENTLY)

4   *Take a Position of Authority*   77

5   *Use Corporal Punishment Wisely*   97

6   *Use Other Consequences*   112

7   *Talk Before Changing How You Discipline*   119

PART III: CREATE A CLIMATE OF GROWTH

8   *Cultivate Character Development*   129

9   *Encourage Responsible Behavior*   140

10   *Develop Each Child's Talents and Intellect*   147

11   *Prepare for Marriage and Sex*   159

12   *Change Approaches with Teenagers*   168

More Resources   179

Preface

My wife Skeeter and I are the parents of three grown sons. Our oldest, Zachary, was two years old when we became Christians. We had brought him up in a totally permissive manner. As a result, he had become a temper tantrum-throwing tyrant who ran the home.

After we surrendered our lives to Christ and began to read the Bible, we became aware that we had much to unlearn and much to learn. We made many mistakes along the way, but with God's help we slowly learned how to be nurturing yet in control, and we learned how to create a Christ-centered home.

When I entered the counseling field, I first worked with children who had histories of delinquent behavior, hyperactivity, property destruction, fire setting, severe emotional disturbances and learning problems. I quickly found that a permissive approach didn't work any better with them than it did with my own son. Again, I realized I had a lot to learn.

You too may have discovered that some of your parenting techniques don't get the results you hoped for. Don't give up. Whether you are married or single, in these pages you will learn how to bring up children who know God's Word and are obedient, respectful, creative, loving and happy.

You can be sure of this because this book is based on the Bible. God's ways work. You will be joining countless other parents who have discovered the joy of putting God's practical biblical principles into practice.

May the Lord richly bless your family as you study.

Doug Britton

Introduction

If you have read many books about parenting, you may feel hopelessly confused by the numerous conflicting theories. It's hard to know whom to believe.

Yet there is a dependable source to which we can go, one proven trustworthy and constant throughout history—the Word of God.

 All Scripture is God-breathed and is useful for teaching, rebuking, correcting and training in righteousness, so that the man of God may be thoroughly equipped for every good work (2 Timothy 3:16-17).

For the word of God is living and active. Sharper than any double-edged sword, it penetrates even to dividing soul and spirit, joints and marrow; it judges the thoughts and attitudes of the heart (Hebrews 4:12).

The Bible covers it all, including nurturing, communication, forgiveness and discipline. God invented the family. He knows how to make it work. That's why *Successful Christian Parenting* is based on the Word of God, taking its ageless truths and showing how to apply them in your family.

Who can use this book?

This book will help both married couples and single parents. It is primarily written for parents of children ages 1-12, yet most of the principles also apply to parents of teenagers.

Getting the Most from this Book

Let me encourage you to *study* and apply this material, not simply skim these pages. I know how easy it is to pick up a book and flip through it, looking for new ideas. That wouldn't help you nearly as much as thoroughly reading all the way through.

Parenting is hard work. Let me encourage you to be willing to put a lot into it—and to do it God's way. Just doing what comes naturally often means repeating our parents' mistakes. We need to approach the subject as students who want to learn from God's Word.

Each chapter presents biblical truths. Don't take them lightly, picking what you like and ignoring the rest. If you skip some chapters, you run the danger of missing out on the insights you need the most.

To get the greatest possible benefit from this book:

Go to the Bible.

Look up all the scriptural references and memorize key verses. There is tremendous power in knowing and applying the Word of God.

For the word of God is living and active. Sharper than any double-edged sword, it penetrates even to dividing soul and spirit, joints and marrow; it judges the thoughts and attitudes of the heart (Hebrews 4:12).

Be an active reader.

Think about and meditate on the material as you read. The more you dig into the material, the more you will grow in wisdom and the ability to become the parent God wants you to be.

- **Pray to change as you study.**

- Underline key points as you read.

- Answer each question.

- Write notes in the margins.

- Talk with friends about insights that speak to you.

Practice what you learn.

Roll up your sleeves and go to work. Apply what you learn. Do not just read about God's principles. That would be like studying nutrition but refusing to eat vegetables.

Paul emphasized this when he wrote, *"Whatever you have learned or received or heard from me, or seen in me—put it into practice" (Philippians 4:9).* James made the same point in James 1:22-25.

As you study, periodically review previous chapters to remind yourself of the lessons you learned.

Give yourself time to change.

You may be able to read this book in a matter of hours, but you never could put it into practice that quickly. Try not to be overwhelmed by the number of changes facing you.

Do not expect overnight changes. God performs miracles, but growth usually is a slower process. Choose a few things to work on, and then add more later. *As you apply his principles, you will see results.*

Do not give up when there are setbacks.

As you study and apply the principles in this book, there may be setbacks, times when you fail. If this happens, don't give up. Learn from your mistakes and press on.

 Not that I have already obtained all this, or have already been made perfect, but I press on to take hold of that for which Christ Jesus took hold of me. Brothers, I do not consider myself yet to

*have taken hold of it. But one thing I do: Forget-
ting what is behind and straining toward what is
ahead, I press on toward the goal to win the prize
for which God has called me heavenward in
Christ Jesus (Philippians 3:12-14).*

If you are a married couple, work as a team.

Do your best to work as a team if you are a married couple. You will find practical ideas about how to do so throughout the book.

 *Personal Application*

Which of the guidelines in "Getting the Most from this
Book" will help you the most?

How will you remind yourself of them?

Turn to the Source of All Truth

Since this book is based on the Bible, it will make the most sense if you know Jesus Christ as your Savior. In other words, if you are a Christian.

A surprising number of people have no idea what it means to be a Christian. For many years, I didn't either. As I grew up, I could see that something was drastically wrong with almost everyone I knew. I never saw the quality of love and trust between people that I felt should be there. I did not observe this lack in others only. I knew that something was missing in me. I explored different philosophies, schools of psychology, sociological approaches, metaphysical ideas and religions. Many sounded reasonable at first, but as I evaluated their reality in my life and in the lives of those who embraced them, they seemed hollow.

I thought there was a spiritual element to life, but couldn't figure out what it was. But God was faithful. Following a series of unexpected events, both Susan and I surrendered our lives to Jesus Christ and were "born again" (John 3:3-7).

As I grew in my Christian walk, I learned about original sin, the sin of Adam and Eve that cripples us all. Here, finally, was an explanation that rang true, a reason for the "something wrong" I had observed and experienced. To my delight, I finally began to see this "something wrong" in me changing for the better. I still have a long way to go, but I am thankful for the work God has done so far.

Jesus offers each of us a walk with God and a fullness of life that is not possible without him. He said, *"I tell you the truth, no one can see the kingdom of God unless he is born again" (John 3:3).* He also said, *"I am the bread of life" (John 6:35),* and *"I am the way and the truth and the life. No one comes to the Father except through me" (John 14:6).*

How does one become a Christian? Paul wrote:

If you confess with your mouth, "Jesus is Lord," and believe in your heart that God raised him from the dead, you will be saved. For it is with your heart that you believe and are justified, and it is with your mouth that you confess and are saved (Romans 10:9-10).

"Believe" means to "adhere to, trust in, and rely on the truth" (Amplified Bible). Becoming a Christian is not simply joining a church or acting religious. It is surrendering your life to Christ and allowing his Spirit to dwell within you.

Do not assume you are a Christian because of your background or church membership. Being raised by Christians does not automatically make you a Christian, nor does going to church, seeking to live a moral life, serving as an elder or leading as a pastor. What counts is whether you have given your life to Jesus Christ.

If you have never done so, I invite you to present yourself to him now, for *"everyone who calls on the name of the Lord will be saved" (Romans 10:13).* Surrender your life to God by accepting Jesus as your Savior and Lord. Then allow God to begin the process of transforming you into the best man or woman, and best husband or wife, you can be.

Personal Application

Have you surrendered your life to Christ? If not, read the following as a prayer:

"Dear Lord, I confess that I am a sinner. Please forgive my sins and accept me as your child. I invite you to be my Savior and the Lord of my life. I surrender myself to you in the name of Jesus Christ, my Savior and Lord."

If you prayed with sincerity, Christ accepted you into his Kingdom and you are now a Christian. Welcome to the family of God!

I accepted Jesus Christ as my Savior and Lord today. Thank you, Jesus!

_____   _____
Signature   Date

As you grow in him, God will transform your life. You have an exciting life ahead of you. These four suggestions will help you get started in your Christian walk:

- Tell someone that you accepted Christ.
- Read the Bible daily, starting with the Gospel of John in the New Testament.
- Join a Bible-believing church.
- Pray regularly.

If You Teach a Parenting Class

Although this book can be studied by an individual or a couple, it also can be taught in a group or class setting. One approach could be to study one chapter per week. (If you want, you can spend two weeks per chapter for a more in-depth study). I suggest one additional week at the beginning of the class for introductions, to go over the Preface and Introduction, and to distribute books.

Start and end each class with prayer.
We need God's assistance. Ask him to help every parent in the class.

Consider breaking into small discussion groups.

If you are teaching a large class, from time to time you may want to break it down into smaller groups of three to five people.

If you do this, assign a leader in each group. If you don't, groups may not stay focused, or one person may do all the talking. You can appoint the leader in a friendly, informal way, such as asking the couple whose anniversary is coming up next to lead. Ask each leader to:

- Start and end the discussion with prayer.

- Keep discussions focused on the topic.

- Make sure each person has time to talk.

Generate group discussion.

Ask questions to generate discussion, either within the total group or smaller groups. You could base some questions on the "Personal Application" sections found in each chapter. You also could ask open-ended questions such as:

- ✓ *"Which of these points most applies to you? Why?"* (Not, "Do any of these points apply to you?")

- ✓ *"What do you think about ...[a principle discussed in the chapter]?"* (Not, "Do you agree with this?" Or, "Does anyone have any comments?")

- ✓ *"How does this section affect you?"*

- ✓ *"What did you learn from this section?"*

- ✓ *"Which of these points do you need to work on?"*

- ✓ *"Which point in this chapter spoke to you the most?"*

Emphasize homework.

Encourage everyone to read the following chapter and answer the questions before coming to the next class.

Give parents some time alone before closing.

Leave a few minutes at the end of class for each couple to privately discuss how they will apply what they have learned. Single parents could get together to share at this time.

Part I:
Create a
Nurturing Home

1. Communicate with Respect and Love

2. Center Your Home in the Lord

3. Care for Yourself and Your Marriage

Chapter 1
Communicate with Respect and Love

The mouth of the righteous is a fountain of life (Proverbs 10:11).

Many parents make the mistake of thinking the key to raising their children is a combination of orders, rules, expectations and punishment. The result in many families is a grim atmosphere, upset parents and resentful children.

Your relationship with your children is the key to how successful you will be as a parent. Orders, rules, expectations and punishment are important, but they backfire if they are your primary approach to bringing up your children.

To be a successful parent, to truly impact the heart of your children for good, you first must establish a warm, loving relationship. Make it your goal to develop a supportive family atmosphere, one in which your children feel secure and protected in your love.

 A happy heart makes the face cheerful, but heartache crushes the spirit (Proverbs 15:13).

Dear children, let us not love with words or tongue but with actions and in truth (1 John 3:18).

Personal Application

Describe the atmosphere in your house. Is it friendly or grim? What are your typical interactions with your children?

_____

God calls both parents to be gentle and loving.

Both parents are responsible to develop a warm and supportive family atmosphere. Let's take a look at how Paul described the way mothers are supposed to act:

 We were gentle among you, like a mother caring for her little children (1 Thessalonians 2:7).

The father also is called on to be a nurturing parent. God wants dads to be gentle and loving—not gruff army drill sergeants. Take a look at the words Paul used to describe a good father:

 For you know that we dealt with each of you as a father deals with his own children, encour-

aging, comforting and urging you to live lives worthy of God, who calls you into his kingdom and glory (1 Thessalonians 2:11-12).

How nurturing are you?

Rate yourself from 0 to 10 on each of the following points.

- "0" means, "I don't do this."
- "10" means, "I do this a lot."

My score (0-10)

I talk with the kids a lot in a friendly way .... ____
I play with them .... ____
I encourage and comfort them .... ____
I help them learn how to do chores .... ____
I tell them I love them .... ____
I comfort them when they are hurt .... ____
I help with their homework .... ____
I help them prepare for bedtime .... ____
I tell them a nighttime story .... ____
I am patient with them .... ____

 *Personal Application*

Select one point in the above quiz on which you scored yourself seven or lower and write your plans to change.

Be Positive

The world is full of problems, disappointments and tragedies. Your children, spouse, boss, neighbor and pastor are imperfect. (So are you!). If you aren't careful, you can find yourself always commenting about negatives things, unaware of the positive things around you.

It's easy to catch your children being bad. It's harder, but more important, to catch them being good.

 Finally, brothers, whatever is true, whatever is noble, whatever is right, whatever is pure, whatever is lovely, whatever is admirable—if anything is excellent or praiseworthy—think about such things (Philippians 4:8).

Look for and comment on the positive.

Many parents tend to specialize in instructing, ordering, nagging, criticizing, threatening and punishing. If this describes you, let me suggest you make it your personal goal to make sure that at least 80-90% of your communications are positive (praise, encouragement or appreciation) or neutral. (normal conversation).

Let me add that it's also appropriate and necessary to bring up problems from time to time. But you can make a tremendous difference in the atmosphere of your home if you mainly comment on positive things.

Say words of praise.

Your praise can have a powerful encouraging effect upon your children.

Place notes that say "PC" above each door.

If you have trouble remembering to praise your children, notes that say "PC" (for "Praise Children") will remind you.

Go easy on including criticism when you praise.

Some parents frequently respond to their children's efforts by saying they could have done more or better. This can be very discouraging.

"I could never do anything to my parents' satisfaction," is a common thing I hear from adults with whom I am counseling.

Do not expect perfection! Your children will think they never are good enough and will carry a sense of inadequacy or fear of trying into adulthood.

 *Personal Application*

Do you need to be more positive when you talk?
❑ Yes ❑ No

If you answered "yes," write a prayer asking God to help you be more positive.

Write a plan to praise your children for something today.

Speak Courteously

The way we speak often is more important than whether we are right or wrong in what we are saying. Always speak in love.

The mouth of the righteous is a fountain of life (Proverbs 10:11).

The tongue of the righteous is choice silver (Proverbs 10:20).

A word aptly spoken is like apples of gold in settings of silver (Proverbs 25:11).

Talk with a friendly tone of voice.
Listen to yourself when you speak. Do you sound friendly or do you sound irritated or angry?

Be aware of your emotions.
Understand what's going on in your mind and do not let your emotions control you. If you are tired, grouchy or sick, watch how you speak. Likewise, if you are a woman who has trouble with PMS, monitor yourself during those times of the month.

Use ten special phrases.
These phrases can help develop a gracious home environment. Use them yourself. Train your children to use them.

✓ "I love you."

✓ "Yes (okay)."

✓ "Please."

✓ "Thank you."

✓ "I'm sorry."

✓ "I was wrong."

✓ "Please forgive me."

✓ "I forgive you."

✓ "How can I help?"

✓ "I would be glad to."

 *Personal Application*

Do you need to speak more courteously to your children? ❑ Yes ❑ No

If you answered "yes," what habit will you work on overcoming?

Listen to Your Children

Very little beats the joy of a good discussion with your children. On the other hand, the heartache of little communication or poor communication devastates many parents. Listening opens the door to good conversations.

 Everyone should be quick to listen, slow to speak and slow to become angry (James 1:19).

Allow your children to express personal feelings.

Be careful not to cut off communication by interrupting, criticizing, ridiculing, or yelling if your children express an opinion you think is wrong.

If your children criticize you or disagree with you:

- Teach them how to do so respectfully, and at appropriate times.

- Be ready to apologize or change; do not be defensive.

- Lovingly express your own opinion or conclusion. (Even though you want to respect your children by listening, you still have final authority!)

Listen to your children's feelings, not just words.

Make it a goal to deeply understand what your children are feeling.

Clarify what your children are saying.

Communication is imprecise. We might be sure we understand what someone is saying, yet be wrong. Here are some ways to make sure you are hearing accurately:

- Rephrase what you think your child said. Ask if you got it right.

- Ask clarifying questions (but do not ask them in a "put-down" manner).

- Gently say what your child's feelings appear to be. Ask if you are correct.

 *Personal Application*

What is one message one of your children has been trying to communicate to you?

How well have you given the message that you understand?

Express Love to Your Children

Frequently tell your children, "I love you and I appreciate you." Don't be stingy with hugs. Make sure your children experience your love every day.

 *Personal Application*

What is one thing you will do today to express love to your children?

Show Respect for Your Children

Remember that your children are human beings. Even if they don't seem to have "earned" respect, treat them with respect. It will have an impact.

Speak respectfully.

Do not call your children names. Never say words along the lines of:

- ✓ "Where are your brains, you dummy?"
- ✓ "Baby."
- ✓ "Stupid."
- ✓ "Liar."
- ✓ "Thief."
- ✓ "Loser."
- ✓ "Cry baby."
- ✓ "I can't believe you did such an idiotic thing."
- ✓ "You're going to get pregnant, just like your aunt."

Demonstrate an interest in their activities.

Attend your children's sports games and other activities.

Show an interest in their problems.

Be willing to listen and talk, even if your children's problems seem minor to you.

Do not ridicule their efforts.

Applaud efforts, even if they are unsuccessful.

Avoid inappropriate humor and teasing.

Put-down jokes hurt children. Although you may think your jokes are harmless fun, your children may be devastated inside—even if they are laughing outside.

Do not attack their character.

Do not "put down" your children or say such things as, "You're no good," or, "You'll never amount to anything".

Discontinue baby talk and childish nicknames.

As your children get older, let them grow up.

Do not compare children to each other.

Support each one; do not show favoritism. Also don't compare them to other people's children.

Do not say, "You always" or "You never."

These words can wound deeply, for they almost always are exaggerations.

 *Personal Application*

Do you sometimes act or speak disrespectfully to your children? ❑ Yes ❑ No

If so, what is one way you have done so?

How will you make up for this?

Spend Time Daily with Each Child

Many parents, especially fathers, spend little time with their children. This also is a problem with mothers who have a job outside the home.

Do your children have to misbehave to get your attention? Show your children that they are important. Spend quality time each day.

- Visit every day after school or when you come home from work.

- If you have more than one child, spend one-to-one time with each child individually as well as with all of them as a group.

- Mothers, if possible, should stay home with young children (1 Timothy 5:14 and Titus 2:4-5). If this isn't possible, don't feel guilty.

Have fun together.

Play games. Have family nights. Playfully wrestle (without getting rough).

 A cheerful heart is good medicine, but a crushed spirit dries up the bones (Proverbs 17:22).

Go on camping trips as a family.

Many families have discovered that they bond more closely when they go camping. We went backpacking with our children from a young age. These outings provided time to play and talk without the distractions found at home. These became special times to all of us and formed many good memories.

Develop family traditions.
Make your own traditions. For example, have a picnic at the zoo the last day of school.

Have "kid's day" once a year.
This is a special day in which your children can plan the activities.

 *Personal Application*

How much individual time do you spend with each child in the average day?

If you would like to increase this time, what will you do this week?

_____

Establish special times of warmth.
There are special times each day during which you can establish a friendly, positive atmosphere:

- **When your children get up**
  Greet your children with friendly words.

- **Meals**
  Eat together as a family and make meals fun. Turn off the TV and visit. Pray for wisdom to avoid problems in these three areas:

  ✓ **Teach manners, but don't overdo it.**
  It's okay to teach basic manners, but do not turn your meals into a battleground over them! One idea: Have one "formal meal" a week at which "company manners" are practiced.

  ✓ **Avoid discussing personal problems.**
  Avoid discussing your children's problems while eating. Save these talks for private times.

  ✓ **Do not make your children eat everything**
  We had our children eat two or three mouthfuls of new foods. Generally, however, we didn't force them to "clean their plates." When they didn't eat everything they usually didn't get dessert.

- **Before and after school**
  Send your children off to school with friendly words. Likewise, greet them warmly when they return.

- **Bedtime**
  Develop routines. Both of us spent time with our children after they went to bed, sometimes together, sometimes taking turns. Our bedtime routine was to:

  ✓ **Have a friendly talk.**

  ✓ **Tell a story.**

   ✓ **Pray.**

   ✓ **Sing a song.**

 *Personal Application*

My plans to establish a bedtime routine:

_____

How to Get Communication Going

If you do not have a pattern of talking with your children, it may feel intimidating when you try to think of a way to get started. Here are some ideas:

Study and practice the previous points.

If you listen and speak courteously, your children may be more likely to want to talk.

Be truly available.
Evaluate yourself. Are you approachable? Respond when your children ask you something.

Do not try to force meaningful conversations.
Allow your child to have some secret thoughts.

Ask questions about things of interest to your kids.
For example, if your children go to school, ask what they did during recess.

Ask your children how you could improve.
Ask what changes they would like to see you make as a parent. Also ask what things they like. Do not get defensive, angry or sorry for yourself because of your children's comments.

Enter your children's world.
Be present when your children skateboard, play video games, etc. Watch. Admire. Join in if you are invited. Develop a bond of shared interests that can lead to more communication.

Do projects together.
People often find themselves talking while working on jigsaw puzzle, cooking, gardening or engaging in other projects.

There is a value in silence.
Turn off the television. Someone might talk!

Apologize and ask forgiveness.
Apologizing opens doors.

🖋 *Personal Application*

If you would like to talk more with your children, choose one of the above ideas and write it here.

Chapter 2

Center Your Home in the Lord

Unless the Lord builds the house, its builders labor in vain (Psalm 127:1).

Probably nothing is more important to you than for your children (1) to be born again and (2) to live their lives according to God's Word. This chapter will present many things you can do to create a Christ-centered home and help your children see what it means to be Christians.

 As for me and my house, we will serve the Lord (Joshua 24:15).

 *Personal Application*

What are your spiritual goals for your children?

Both parents are responsible for spiritual training.

Notice in the following verse that God gives both father and mother the responsibility to instruct their children in God's truth.

> *Listen, my son, to your father's instruction and do not forsake your mother's teaching (Proverbs 1:8).*

Evaluate yourself.

How involved are you with your children's spiritual upbringing? Rate yourself from 0 to 10 on each of the following points.

- "0" means, "I don't do this much at all."
- "10" means, "I do this a lot."

My score (0-10)

I pray with the children regularly .... _____
I talk with them about God throughout the day .... _____
I set a good example with my church attendance .... _____
I help them get ready for church .... _____
I talk with them about their church activities .... _____
I take them to special church events .... _____
I tell them about sharing Jesus with others .... _____
I lead family or individual Bible studies. .... _____

Personal Application

Do you need to be more actively involved in your children's spiritual lives? ❑ Yes ❑ No

If you answered "yes," what areas do you think God would want you to change?

Avoid Common Parental Mistakes

Parents sometimes sabotage their own efforts to encourage their children to draw close to God. The following guidelines will help you avoid making common mistakes.

Do not overemphasize rules.

Many parents present Christianity as a list of things to do and not to do. It's true that the Bible gives us rules to follow, but the most important thing by far is for us to be born again and to enter into an individual relationship with God.

Present Christianity positively, as something to be desired, not as a grim religion with a lot of rules.

 Taste and see that the Lord is good (Psalm 34:8).

Practice what you preach.

Many children comment that their parents pressure them to act like Christians, yet the parents act just the opposite. If you act like a loving, respectful person at church, act the same in the car and at home. If you tell your children not to be angry, don't display anger yourself.

> *Why do you look at the speck of sawdust in your brother's eye and pay no attention to the plank in your own eye? How can you say to your brother, "Let me take the speck out of your eye," when all the time there is a plank in your own eye? You hypocrite, first take the plank out of your own eye, and then you will see clearly to remove the speck from your brother's eye (Matthew 7:3-5).*

Don't depend on the church for spiritual instruction.

Some people think the church has all the responsibility to provide their children's spiritual training, yet that's not how God set things up. The church plays an important role, yet the parents have the primary responsibility. The Bible says you are to instruct your children and talk about God's Word *"when you sit at home and when you walk along the road, when you lie down and when you get up" (Deuteronomy 6: 7).*

Personal Application

Do you make any of these mistakes? ❑ Yes ❑ No

If so, which ones?

Invite God Into *All* Your Interactions

Throughout the day, relate scriptural principles to your life circumstances and those that are faced by your children.

These commandments that I give you today are to be on your hearts. Impress them on your children. Talk about them when you sit at home and when you walk along the road, when you lie down and when you get up. Tie them as symbols on your hands and bind them on your foreheads. Write them on the door frames of your houses and on your gates (Deuteronomy 6:6-9).

Fix these words of mine in your hearts and minds; tie them as symbols on your hands and bind them on your foreheads. Teach them to your children, talking about them when you sit at home and lie down and when you get up. Write them on the doorframes of your houses and on your gates (Deuteronomy 11:18-20).

Fill your home with Christian books and posters.

The *Chronicles of Narnia* by C.S. Lewis, *The Treekeepers* by Susan McGee Britton (also known as "Skeeter"—my wife) and *Little Pilgrim's Progress* are excellent children's books.

Fellowship with other Christians in your home.

Look for those who will include your children in conversations. This helps your children develop a sense of Christian community.

Handle holidays in a Christian manner.

Look for activities to glorify Jesus at Christmas and Easter. If you have a Christmas tree, do not "worship" it. (The tree in Jeremiah 10:3-4 sounds like the Christmas tree in many homes.)

Do not tell your children that Santa Claus, the Easter bunny and the tooth fairy are real. If you say they are real, when your children grow older and learn better, they may decide that Jesus, too, is only a nice story figure.

If you include these figures in your celebrations, identify them as make-believe. Fantasy can be fun, but be sure to identify it as fantasy.

If you have told your children that these figures are real, meet with them, tell the truth, and explain why you played that game with them. Ask their forgiveness.

Do not allow demon-oriented play at Halloween.

Sing as a family.

Make it a tradition to sing worship songs in the car and at other times.

> *Speak to one another with psalms, hymns and spiritual songs. Sing and make music in your heart to the Lord (Ephesians 5:19).*

Play Bible games.

Check out age-appropriate Bible games in the local Bible bookstore.

Play Christian CDs and videotapes that they enjoy.

Numerous excellent resources are available.

 *Personal Application*

What is one way you already invite God into your daily interactions?

What is one more way you will invite the Lord into your daily activities?

Provide a Godly Example

Are you a Christian? Is Jesus truly your Lord day-to-day? How do you act when you are out of church? Regardless of what you say, your example is what really counts! You are "known and read" by your children (2 Corinthians 3:2-3).

> *I have been reminded of your sincere faith, which first lived in your grandmother Lois and in your mother Eunice and, I am persuaded, now lives in you also (2 Timothy 1:5).*

What do your children see you doing?
Evaluate yourself using the following points.

- **Are you a Christian?**

- **Do you have a gentle manner?**
  Do you handle anger or frustrations in a godly manner? Do you love your enemies? Do you pray for those who despitefully use you? Do you show patience? Do you yell a lot? Do you swear?

Let your gentleness be evident to all. The Lord is near (Philippians 4:5).

- **Do you read the Bible daily?**

- **Do you pray daily?**

- **Do you tithe?**

- **Do you thank God?**
  Do you give God credit for victories?

Always giving thanks to God the Father for everything, in the name of our Lord Jesus Christ (Ephesians 5:20).

- **Do you show a genuine concern about others?**
  When you talk about people, is it with love and concern, or do you complain and gossip? Are you developing your own personal ministry?

- **Do you tell others about Christ?**

- **Do you praise God daily?**

On my bed I remember you; I think of you through the watches of the night (Psalm 63:6).

Let them praise the name of the Lord, for his name alone is exalted; his splendor is above the earth and the heavens (Psalm 148:13).

Let the saints rejoice in this honor and sing for joy on their beds (Psalm 149:5).

- **Do you keep your word?**

- **Do you lust after material things?**

- **Do you watch questionable movies?**

- **Do you dwell on positive things?**
  Or do you dwell on the negative? Do you worry, or do you trust God? Study Philippians 4:4-8.

- **Do you follow the speed limit?**

- **Do you admit your mistakes?**
  When you make a mistake, do you admit it and ask forgiveness?

- **Do you demonstrate love?**
  Is love the supreme message in your home? Write out 1 Corinthians 13:4-8 and put it on your refrigerator door.

Love is patient, love is kind. It does not envy, it does not boast, it is not proud. It is not rude, it is not self-seeking, it is not easily angered, it keeps no record of wrongs. Love does not delight in evil but rejoices with the truth. It always protects, always trusts, always hopes, always perseveres. Love never fails (1 Corinthians 13:4-8).

Personal Application

If someone asked your children if they wanted to be like you, what would they say?

Are you the type of person you would like your children to be? Why or why not?

Write a prayer asking God to help you make any needed changes in your life.

Pray *with* Your Children

When you pray with your children, you are introducing them to one of the greatest privileges we have—to communicate with God, our Creator.

Most of us, including our children, tend to think praying is a time to ask God for something. That's one aspect of prayer, but there are other elements. One key is to give thanks for his love and the good things we experience in life.

When should you pray with your children?

Make a pattern of praying at special times throughout the day.

- **Pray before meals.**

    Jesus gave us an example when he gave thanks before eating (Matthew 14:19).

- **Pray before school.**

    Before our boys went to school, Skeeter prayed for them, borrowing from the following verses.

 Jesus grew in wisdom and stature, and in favor with God and men (Luke 2:52).

I keep asking that the God of our Lord Jesus Christ, the glorious Father, may give you the Spirit of wisdom and revelation, so that you may know him better. I pray also that the eyes of your heart may be enlightened in order that you may know the hope to which he has called you, the riches of his glorious inheritance in the saints, and his incomparably great power for us who believe. That power is like the working of his mighty strength, which he exerted in Christ when he raised him from the dead and seated him at his right hand in the heavenly realms, far above all rule and authority, power and dominion, and every title that can be given, not only in the present age but also in the one to come. And God placed all things under his feet and appointed him to be head over everything for the church, which is his body, the fullness of him who fills everything in every way (Ephesians 1:17-23).

Also ask your children to pray for you before school. This can be a real blessing for them and for you.

- **Pray at bedtime.**

- **Pray at times of need, or when a child is hurt.**

Teach your children how to pray.

Children's "natural" prayers often are self-centered. The following are ways to teach your children to pray.

- Have them pray out loud.

- Teach them to pray for others' needs (including yours).

- Teach them to give thanks.

- Teach them the Lord's Prayer (Matthew 6:9-13). Discuss what it means.

 *Personal Application*

What are your plans to pray with your children?

Pray (and Fast) *for* Your Children

We often think our words are the most valuable gift we can give our children. Yet our prayers are much more important. Pray for your children daily.

 *Personal Application*

If you don't already pray for your children each day, write a plan for when you will do so.

_____

Talk about God with Your Children

When you talk, "share" instead of lecturing. Although sometimes it's appropriate to teach authoritatively, it can become boring to your children to have to sit and listen to you lecture on and on and on.

Instead, tell how a Scripture applies to you or what God showed you during the day. Tell how the Lord helped you with a problem. Encourage your children to discuss how the Scriptures apply to their real life.

Do not overreact to provocative statements.

If one of your children says he or she disagrees with a church doctrine, does not believe in God or is uncertain about the truth of the Bible, respond courteously and wisely.

- *Share* your beliefs, but do not argue.

- Recognize with your child that he or she must make a personal decision about how to respond to God's love gift of Jesus Christ.

- Suggest that your child pray and ask God to help with his or her unbelief.

- Do not give your child the message that you are "thrown."

- Do not give angry speeches.

- Show respect for your child's statements, even if you disagree with them.

Allow and encourage questions.

Admit it when you do not understand something.

Help your children put a question "on the shelf," waiting for future understanding.

When appropriate, say, "I'll study that and report back." Be sure to follow up.

Discuss various interpretations of Bible passages.

You can say what you believe about them, and why.

Personal Application

What is one thing you will share about your Christian walk with your children this week? When will you do it?

Introduce Your Children to the Lord

As I wrote at the beginning of the chapter, there's nothing more important than developing a personal relationship with God through his Son Jesus Christ. Jesus himself said the most important commandment is to love God.

Love the Lord your God with all your heart and with all your soul and with all your mind and with all your strength (Mark 12:30).

Salvation is a personal experience.

Do not assume your children are Christians because they were brought up in a Christian home.

Lead each child through a personal "sinner's prayer," confessing his or her sins and inviting Jesus to be his or her Savior and Lord.

Remember that salvation is a work of the Spirit.
It is something that God does. You can present God's plan of salvation to each child, but then it is between him and your child. Do not try to force your children to acknowledge Jesus as Lord.

 *Personal Application*

Are you sure your children have been born again?
❑ Yes ❑ No

If you aren't sure, pray for the right opportunity to share Jesus' plan of salvation with them.

Teach about Their Identity in Christ

Many of our problems as adults stem from not grasping who we are in Christ. We can prepare a wonderful foundation for our children by helping them learn their identity, purpose and power in Christ. Look for ways to develop these themes as you talk and pray with your children.

Help them understand their identity in Christ.

Once we are born again, we become children of the living God. It is this relationship that should define your children's identity, not their attractiveness, skills or intelligence. Let them know they are *"seated with him in the heavenly places"* *(Ephesians 2:6).*

 You received the Spirit of sonship (Romans 8:15).

We are God's children (Romans 8:16).

For God so loved the world that he gave his only begotten Son that whoever believes in him shall not perish but have eternal life (John 3:16).

Also study Galatians 4:5-7.

Help them understand their purpose.

God has a purpose for each of them regardless of their fame or position.

 For we are God's workmanship, created in Christ Jesus to do good works, which God prepared in advance for us to do (Ephesians 2:10).

God has given each of our children talents or abilities he wants them to develop. More importantly, he wants them to be his ambassadors, touching their world for Christ.

Help them understand their power in Christ.

Help your children know they are *"more than conquerors through him"* *(Romans 8:37).*

 *Personal Application*

How well do you think your children understand who they are in Christ? Write any steps you could take to help them better grasp the truth.

Have Family Bible Studies

It is important that your children learn and apply the Bible in their lives. Many children never mature in their faith. When they get older, they leave what they think is their "childish religion" of rituals and rules behind and adopt un-christian approaches to the world. We need to help them grow in faith, knowledge and maturity through study of the Word.

The Scriptures tell us to study the Bible.

 Do not let this Book of the Law depart from your mouth; meditate on it day and night, so that you may be careful to do everything written in it.

Then you will be prosperous and successful (Joshua 1:8).

But his delight is in the law of the Lord, and on his law he meditates day and night (Psalm 1:2).

Also read Psalm 12:6, 78:1-8, 119:11; Isaiah 40:8; Matthew 4:4 and John 8:31-32.

The Bible is God's Word.

 All Scripture is God-breathed and is useful for teaching, rebuking, correcting and training in righteousness (2 Timothy 3:16).

For prophecy never had its origin in the will of man, but men spoke from God as they were carried along by the Holy Spirit (2 Peter 1:21).

You can lead a Bible study!

The following system for Bible study is simple. You can do it even if you don't know the Bible very well.

Bible study guidelines

The following guidelines and suggested steps are for family Bible studies. In addition to these family studies, you may also want to have individual studies with each child.

- Give each child a Bible he or she can understand. Be sure your children are able to understand what they are reading! (Children often learn "memory verses" without understanding what they mean!) Use Bibles or small Bible storybooks with lots of pictures if you have young children.

- Set a specific, regular time for your family Bible study each day.

- Study a short passage ahead of time so you will be prepared. Do not make the studies too long.

- Initially, study short sections of Scripture. Go through one book of the Bible day by day instead of turning to random verses each day.

- If there is a wide difference in your children's ages, it probably would be best to have separate Bible studies for different age groups.

- Keep a balance between "doctrinal" and "personal application" studies.

- Take turns sharing leadership once you have developed a Bible study routine. Your children will benefit from taking the leadership role!

- With very young children, do not try to apply the following steps. Instead, lead them through simple stories yourself. Point to pictures and tell the story in your own words.

Suggested steps to follow in your Bible study

- Take turns being the leader. Give your children opportunities to lead as they grow older.

- The leader asks someone to pray for God's blessing on the study.

- The leader then asks someone to read a short passage in Bible.

- The leader asks each person what the passage means, or for something he or she got out of it. Everyone shares what the passage means. (The leader makes sure all talk by asking questions, such as "What do you think this means?" or "What does this mean to you?")

- After everyone else speaks, the leader shares his or her interpretation or personal application.

- The leader asks someone to close the study with prayer.

 *Personal Application*

If you don't already have a regular family Bible study, write plans to start one.

Help Children Benefit from Church

A good beginning point is to be involved in your church yourself. Set a good example.

Teach your children respect and reverence.

Teach them how to act reverently in church. Also help them to speak respectfully about the pastor and church leaders.

How do you talk about the church and its leaders? Your example is very important. Do you express honor and appreciation? Do you frequently complain about the church? If you disagree with something, do you do so respectfully?

Talk with your children about what they learned.

Show an interest in what they learned in church. Also, talk as a family about church sermons. Help your children apply what they learn at church to their real lives.

Get involved with your children's youth programs.

Volunteer to help. Invite leaders to your home for fellowship and dinner.

If your children do not like the pastor or teacher:

- Teach your children to treat their leaders with honor, even those they do not enjoy or those whose teaching they do not find helpful.

- Teach your children how to disagree respectfully. Teach them to dig into the Word and to base their positions on the Word, not just on personal feelings.

- If one of your children has been a Christian a long time and is bored by hearing messages designed for immature Christians:

- Help him or her learn how to glean "nuggets."

- Help your child learn to look for ways to minister to others.

- Encourage your child to worship God and get his or her eyes off people.

• If a child has trouble with a pastor or teacher, it may be appropriate for you to talk with the leader.

- You may be able to help him or her identify ways to minister to your child.

- You may learn about some problems your child is having.

If your children have trouble with other children:

Help them learn to look for ways to minister to other children. A good starting point is to look for someone who appears to be lonely or an outsider and to reach out to that person.

 *Personal Application*

My plans to help my children benefit from church:

Chapter 3

Care for Yourself and Your Marriage

A man ... shall cleave unto his wife (Genesis 2:24, King James Bible).

Children are a blessing from God, yet if you are not careful, you can focus so much attention on them that you neglect yourself and your marriage.

In this chapter, we will look at two areas, caring for yourself and caring for your marriage. Let's start with caring for yourself.

Care for Yourself

Our main task as Christians is to serve others (Matthew 20:26-28, Galatians 5:13 and Philippians 2:5-7). Yet as long as we keep this as our main goal, it's okay also to pay attention to our own interests.

Each of you should look not only to your own interests, but also to the interests of others (Philippians 2:4).

Notice the phrases *"not only"* and *"but also."* Although our primary task is to serve others, these phrases let us know it's okay to pay attention to our own interests.

The following list can give you some ideas about things that are important for you personally.

Develop interests besides your children.

It can be refreshing to spend time reading, gardening, knitting, programming the computer or learning new skills. As you engage in projects or learn more about something, you will find you have more to contribute to your family.

Seek out friendships and fellowship.

Look for friends who will support you in your role as a parent. Also make friends with people who will encourage you as you develop your interests.

Have "personal time" each day.

Go off alone for prayer (Matthew 14:23).

Take time away from your home.

If you can, spend some time without the kids away from the home each week.

Get enough sleep.

Read Psalm 127:2.

Personal Application

Do you need to do more to pay attention to your own interests? ☐ Yes ☐ No

What changes would you like to make? What steps can you take to begin making these changes?

Care for Your Marriage

The Bible says you are *"one flesh"* *(Malachi 2:15 and Mark 10:8)* and you are to cleave unto your spouse (Genesis 2:24, King James Bible). Although you may need to spend more minutes per day with younger children than with your mate, always remember that your marriage is primary. Take care of this precious relationship.

 The man said, "This is now bone of my bones and flesh of my flesh; she shall be called 'woman,' for she was taken out of man." For this reason a man will leave his father and mother and be united to his wife, and they will become one flesh (Genesis 2:23-24).

The Basics

Don't think you are neglecting or harming your children when you put some time into your marriage. A strong marriage is good for you and one of the greatest gifts you can give your children.

Be sensitive to each other's desires.

Serve one another. Identify what's important to your mate and then put effort into those areas.

 Your attitude should be the same as that of Christ Jesus: Who, being in very nature God, did not consider equality with God something to be grasped, but made himself nothing, taking the very nature of a servant, being made in human likeness (Philippians 2:5-7).

Talk privately every day.

Don't let your relationship get stale. Make time to talk privately daily.

Go on dates and vacations as a couple.

Have family activities and vacations, yet also go on dates and short vacations as a couple. Your children will not always live at home. Take time to develop your relationship when the children still live at home. You will be better prepared for the day you have an "empty nest."

 *Personal Application*

When is the last time you went on a date?

What are your spouse's major desires?

Make a plan to fulfill one of these desires in the next four days.

Common Problems Involving Children

A newborn gets almost all the wife's attention.

A mother who has just experienced the miracle of birth is likely to be busy caring for the baby. The husband may feel neglected.

One parent is "too busy" for his or her spouse.

One parent may be *extremely* involved in the children's lives, playing with them, reading to them, helping with homework and taking them to activities. This parent leaves little time for the marriage. In some cases, the mother sleeps with a child instead of her husband.

The wife is worn out.

The mother may be exhausted from caring for the children or cleaning house. She may resent her husband because he does little to help. He, on the other hand, may feel neglected because she does not have time or energy for him.

You disagree about how to raise children.

Disagreements about discipline, bedtime and other issues often produce tension in a marriage. The tension sometimes continues after children leave home, because parents argue about helping adult children who face problems with school, money, drugs, employment or their own marriage.

 *Personal Application*

Does your marriage suffer from problems involving your children? ❑ Yes ❑ No

If so, what are they?

Guidelines with Children

Show that you and your mate are united.

Love your children, but let them know you and your spouse are one flesh and your relationship is very special. Do not say you love them less, but demonstrate that you and your spouse are a unit. Talk and hug in their presence.

Pitch in and help if your mate is stressed and could use support. Present a united front when it comes to rules, structure and discipline.

Support and encourage each other.

Look for ways to help each other with the kids and around the house. Instead of criticizing and complaining, encourage and praise each other. Raising kids is a lot of work and we all need support!

 Do not let any unwholesome talk come out of your mouths, but only what is helpful for building others up according to their needs, that it may benefit those who listen (Ephesians 4:29).

Keep your bedroom private.

Train your children to ask for and receive permission before entering your bedroom.

A baby's father should be understanding.

I still remember the sense of abandonment I felt in the months after our first child was born. I was immature, and felt sorry for myself. It took me some time to learn to be patient, understanding and supportive.

It's natural for a mother to focus most of her attention on a new baby. Not only that, it takes a while for her to recover from childbirth, physically and emotionally. Dad needs to be understanding and get involved in child rearing.

A newborn's mother should be understanding.

Although it's natural for a mother to focus her attention on her new child, she should also give her mate some attention. As the infant grows, she should focus increasingly more attention on her husband.

Do not argue in front of the children.

It's okay to talk about politics, faith or what car to buy when your children are present if you can do so respectfully. This can help them learn how to have mature conversations.

However, save difficult personal discussions until you are out of earshot. Then talk quietly.

Ask your spouse before making family plans.

Confer with your mate before planning trips or giving the kids money. Work as a team.

Don't let your adult children drain you.

Be wise in any help you give adult children. It can be a great joy to help them as they embark on their life adventures. But it can be draining if your children *expect* your help or pressure you to give money. Many couples have spent their retirement funds trying to help adult children who were unthankful and resentful that their parents did not give them more.

The most loving thing in such a situation usually is to cut off the funds and let your children deal with their own problems. If you constantly bail them out, they will not become responsible. Let them know you love them, but do not give in to pressure.

Except for truly exceptional cases, do not give money to an adult child without your spouse's approval. Along the same lines, do not invite an adult child back home unless you and your spouse agree.

Personal Application

What changes do you need to make, if any, in how you apply the above guidelines?

Typical Problems with Stepchildren

If you have a blended family, one with stepchildren, you may have experienced some of the following common problems.

The stepparent is seen as an outsider.

The natural parent and children may have developed an extremely close bond during years of living together. The new spouse may be seen as an outsider by the children, and perhaps a threat to the memory of the absent parent.

The stepparent's efforts to discipline backfire.

The natural parent may have become too permissive with the children, acting more like a friend than a parent. The new spouse may think, "These kids need some discipline," and try to straighten them out. This often results in the natural parent becoming resentful and protective, thinking the new spouse is mean. The stepparent, feeling unsupported, becomes angry and thinks, "It's them against me," or, "My spouse is on their side."

The children try to sabotage the new marriage.

Children may attempt to drive a wedge between their natural parent and their new stepparent. This may be because they hope to get their natural parents back together. They also might try to stir things up because they do not like their new stepparent. Or they may feel jealous of the attention their dad or mom is giving their stepparent.

One spouse appears to favor his or her children.

If one person brings children into the marriage, he or she may seem to spoil them or discipline them more leniently than children his or her spouse brought into the marriage.

One seems to favor children born to the couple.

The spouse who brought children into the marriage may think his or her spouse discriminates against them and favors children born to them as a couple.

A parent seems to spoil his or her visiting children.

When children living out of the home visit for a few days, the natural parent may appear to ignore his or her spouse and allow the children to act out. Or he or she may spend massive amounts of money entertaining them. The stepparent may feel jealous and think, "My spouse loves his (or her) children more than me."

 *Personal Application*

If you are in a blended family, describe the relationships between each spouse and each child.

Guidelines with Stepchildren

If some of the above problems describe your situation, do not be surprised. Similar patterns are repeated over and over, particularly when a man marries a woman who has children. Don't give up. Follow the previous guidelines on dealing with children. In addition, put the following suggestions into practice.

Tell your children your marriage is permanent.

If you are the natural parent, explain to your children that your relationship with your new husband or wife is very special and is permanent. Tell them you love them dearly, but don't give them the message you and they are a special team, and your spouse is an outsider.

Try to understand your spouse's point of view.

If your spouse feels insecure or afraid, reassure him or her instead of getting into a fight.

Develop a relationship with your stepchildren.

Work on being friends with your stepchildren. Understand how difficult it may be for them to bond with you. Make it your main goal to gain a positive relationship with them, not to discipline them. Treat them with love and respect.

Let the birth parent take the lead in disciplining.

Stepparents often move too quickly into a disciplinary role and end up antagonizing the children and spouse. It's usually wiser to let the natural parent take the lead role in discipline.

Follow your spouse's guidelines, even when you are alone with the children. If you think the kids need a more authoritative approach, talk *privately* with your spouse about it. After a period of time, slowly begin to take disciplinary measures, but keep communicating with your spouse.

Support your spouse.

If you are the natural parent and your spouse disciplines your children, do not intervene to protect them unless your mate is truly hurting them. If you intervene, the tension level will probably rise and result in more problems. Instead, privately share your concerns later in the day.

There may be exceptions, but they should be rare. If your mate is about to hurt the children, intervene. If he or she constantly berates them or assigns inappropriate punishment, and doesn't listen to your private communications, step in and take over. If your spouse physically abuses the kids, take action—legal, if necessary.

On a different note, if your children treat your spouse disrespectfully, let them know this is inappropriate and will not be tolerated.

Pray together before children visit.

Before one spouse's children visit, ask God to help both of you to love, have wisdom and act as a team.

Do not "tune out" others when your kids visit.

It is understandable if you want to spend special time with your children after you have been apart, yet also be sensitive to the feelings of your spouse and the other children living in the home.

Be gracious when your spouse's children visit.

Your mate loves his or her children and misses them deeply. It's natural for him or her to want to spend special time with them when they visit. Ask God's help to be free from jealousy, to provide support and to express love to the children.

If it feels like you are in prison when they are in your home, read Paul's words about being *"an ambassador in chains" (Ephesians 6:20)*. He saw his chains as an opportunity to demonstrate the love of Christ.

 *Personal Application*

If you have blended family problems, review the above points and write plans to overcome these problems.

Part II:
Exercise
Authority
(Gently)

4. Take a Position of Authority

5. Use Corporal Punishment Wisely

6. Utilize Other Consequences

7. Talk Before Changing How You Discipline

Chapter 4
Take a Position
of Authority

*Children, obey your parents in the Lord,
for this is right (Ephesians 6:1).*

The Bible tells children to obey their parents. It also lets us know obedience does not come naturally. Children need training.

Both parents are called to roles of authority, to train their children to be respectful and obedient. But in many families, one parent—often the mother—backs away from this role, leaving the other one responsible for all discipline. (In some families these roles are reversed.) Notice in the following verses that God tells children to obey *both* parents.

 Children, obey your parents in the Lord, for this is right (Ephesians 6:1).

The rod of correction imparts wisdom, but a child left to himself disgraces his mother (Proverbs 29:15).

Women who see discipline as the father's responsibility often fear seeming mean and losing their children's love. Sometimes they think they are not emotionally strong enough to deal with a strong-willed child. And sometimes they are actually intimidated by a child. The result? Disrespectful and disobedient children.

✏ *Personal Application*

Do you need to be more authoritative?
❏ Yes   ❏ No

If so, what changes do you think you need to make?

Prepare Yourself Emotionally

Learn to be comfortable being in control. Do not feel guilty. Parents should be in charge, not children. Children need the security and structure of knowing that their parents are in control. It's scary thinking you're in control when you are a child.

Be emotionally prepared for problems.

If you expect perfection, you will be disappointed and upset. When a child does something particularly bad, parents often feel their world has fallen apart. Common reactions:

- Parents feel guilty, or like a failure.

- Parents feel embarrassed.

- Parents feel mad at the child.

- Parents take it personally.

- Parents feel mad at their spouse (or ex-spouse) for not doing enough.

Folly is bound up in the heart of a child (Proverbs 22:15). Expect your children to have problems, no matter how good a parent you are. Adam and Eve had a perfect father, yet they sinned (Genesis 3:6).

When you expect problems, rather than perfection, you are better prepared to deal with the problems.

After all, everyone has problems, including you. There are times in your life when you tried to improve in certain areas, but you failed. This should help you be more understanding toward your children. Although you may need to deal with their problems, you can do so without getting angry.

Along the same lines, don't expect your children to be perfect when they leave home; each child will have things to learn in the future.

Treat negative incidents as learning opportunities.

It's your job to teach your children to be obedient (1 Timothy 3:4-5) and to learn whatever lessons they need to learn. Do not be mad at them because you have to do this. Instead, look upon misbehavior as an opportunity for your children to learn valuable lessons.

The way you respond is important. Approach your task as a God-given responsibility and as an opportunity for your child to learn and grow in wisdom. Remember that you are teaching and training, not just punishing. Act in wisdom and love.

Stay in control if a child is trying to upset you. Do not "take it personally" (even if your child wants you to).

> *Consider it pure joy, my brothers, whenever you face trials of many kinds (James 1:2)*

Accept your responsibility to discipline.

Discipline is part of the parenting process. When your children misbehave, God expects you to discipline them. If you have trouble with the idea of disciplining your children, it can help to remember that God disciplines us.

> *My son, do not despise the Lord's discipline and do not resent his rebuke, because the Lord disciplines those he loves, as a father the son he delights in (Proverbs 3:11-12).*

> *The Lord disciplines those he loves, and he punishes everyone he accepts as a son (Hebrews 12:6).*

> *Those whom I love I rebuke and discipline (Revelation 3:19).*

When you lovingly discipline your children, you set the stage for them to develop self-discipline. When done appropriately, it is a wonderful gift. When done poorly, it is destructive.

Do you have a strong-willed child? With God's help, his or her strong will can be redirected toward righteousness.

Discipline your son, for in that there is hope; do not be a willing party to his death (Proverbs 19:18).

Discipline your son, and he will give you peace; he will bring delight to your soul (Proverbs 29:17).

No discipline seems pleasant at the time, but painful. Later on, however, it produces a harvest of righteousness and peace for those who have been trained by it (Hebrews 12:11).

 *Personal Application*

Do you treat negative incidents as learning opportunities, or does anger control you?

Write how you would like to respond emotionally when your children misbehave. Then pray and ask God to help you act that way.

Avoid Common Mistakes

Let's take a look at some common ways that parents react to disobedience. Notice that these ways are unscriptural and ineffective in the long run.

- Nagging

- Reminding

- Threatening or warning

- Pleading. (Something "democratic" parents often do.)

- Lecturing

- Bribing

- Yelling

- "Counseling"

- Insulting

- Using guilt

- Ignoring

- Committing physical abuse

- Using long-term punishment (restrictions or chores)

- Punishing "creatively" (such as washing a child's mouth out with soap for swearing or biting a child who has bitten you)

✐ Personal Application

Do you make mistakes in any of the above areas?
❑ Yes ❑ No

Which of these mistakes do you make?

_____

Act in Charge

When I first worked with delinquent teenagers, I felt extremely uncomfortable as an authority figure. Yet I learned to overcome my natural feelings and *act* in control.

You can do the same thing as a parent. First, imagine how a mature, comfortable Christian parent would handle the situation. Then pray for God's help and role-play (acting out the role of a mature Christian parent).

 *Personal Application*

Describe how you would like to act when your children misbehave.

_____

Six Keys to Parental Authority

There are six important elements to developing obedience and respect:

1. Cultivate a friendly and respectful relationship.

Let me remind you about the principles from chapters 1 and 2. *Your relationship with your children is the key to your authority.*

A lot of parents make the mistake of acting like an army drill sergeant, constantly giving orders and meting out negative consequences.

That's a bad approach. It may seem to get good results at first. But if you primarily rely on punishment (or the fear of punishment), the eventual result most likely will be outward rebellion or inward resentment in the teenage years, if not earlier.

To be truly effective, discipline must take place within the context of a loving, nurturing relationship. Your home should be a stimulating and fun setting for growth, not a grim battleground. Be careful not to constantly give orders to your children or treat them as servants.

Even though punishment sometimes is necessary, be sure that your interactions with your children are friendly, nurturing and respectful.

If you have not yet read Part I, "Create a Nurturing Home," I urge you to go through those chapters before continuing with this chapter.

2. Teach your children verses that support your role.

Your goals should be for your children to honor you, obey you and learn from you. Teach your children what God says about these three areas.

- **Children are to honor their parents.**

Honor your father and your mother, so that you may live long in the land the Lord your God is giving you (Exodus 20:12).

Honor your father and your mother, as the Lord your God has commanded you, so that you may live long and that it may go well with you in the land the Lord your God is giving you (Deuteronomy 5:16).

"Honor your father and mother"—which is the first commandment with a promise—"that it may go well with you and that you may enjoy long life on the earth" (Ephesians 6:2-3).

- **Children are to obey their parents.**

Children, obey your parents in the Lord, for this is right (Ephesians 6:1).

Children, obey your parents in everything, for this pleases the Lord (Colossians 3:20).

[An overseer] must manage his own family well and see that his children obey him with proper respect (1 Timothy 3:4).

- **Children are to learn from their parents.**

Listen, my sons, to a father's instruction; pay attention and gain understanding. I give you sound learning, so do not forsake my teaching (Proverbs 4:1-2).

A wise son heeds his father's instruction, but a mocker does not listen to rebuke (Proverbs 13:1).

3. Demonstrate a teachable attitude.
When your children see you do the following things, they are more likely to do them, themselves.

- Apologize when you make a mistake.

- Respond appropriately to criticism.

- Let your children know that that you want to improve and that you, too, are working on problems.

Do not do the same things for which you punish your children. Your double standard will speak louder than your punishment. "Do as I say, not as I do" is a terrible message. A bad example: Many parents yell at their children, yet feel free to punish their children for yelling.

Are there other areas in your life that need changing? If your children see you striving to become a better person, they will be likely to follow your example.

4. Teach appropriate behavior.

Reward your children. Do not just punish for inappropriate behavior.

5. Punish your children lovingly.

Remember, you aren't simply punishing, but also are training. Proper discipline helps your children develop godly self-discipline.

Do not humiliate or embarrass your children. For example, do not force your children to wear a "dunce" hat.

Whenever you discipline, do so in love. Chastisement delivered in anger usually has worse results than if you do not chastise at all.

 Brothers, if someone is caught in a sin, you who are spiritual should restore him gently (Galatians 6:1).

Fathers, do not exasperate your children; instead, bring them up in the training and instruction of the Lord (Ephesians 6:4).

6. Gradually become less authoritative over time.

Your goal, as your children grow older, should be for them to assume more and more responsibilities with you giving less and less direct orders. Give them increased responsibility and decision-making authority. Help them learn how to act independently under God's control. (A future chapter covers how to do this.)

 *Personal Application*

Review the above keys to parental authority. Which of them do you think you do well?

Which ones do you think you need to work on?

Expect Obedience

Do your children do what you tell them the first time you say something? Or do you find yourself repeating yourself, nagging, reminding, threatening, pleading, lecturing, bribing or yelling?

A key to successful authority is to train your children to do what you say at your first (quiet) request. If they do not obey, deal with the misbehavior instead of repeating yourself over and over.

You can train your children to do what you say at your first request, your second request or your tenth request. Why not make it the first request?

 *Personal Application*

When you tell your children to do something, do they respond right away? Or do you repeat yourself?

What should you do instead of repeating yourself? (If you aren't sure, keep reading the next three chapters.)

Don't Excuse Misbehavior

The parents of many delinquent children with whom I have counseled automatically protected their children when they got in trouble with school personnel or law enforcement officers. This prevented these children from developing a personal sense of responsibility or accountability.

When you hear a negative report about your child, investigate the facts. If your child has done something wrong, make sure he or she assumes responsibility for his or her behavior.

If a child has been mistreated, help him or her deal with the situation in a mature way.

 *Personal Application*

How would you respond if a child got into trouble with the law or the school?

Supervise Your Children Closely

Pay close attention to what your children are doing. This is especially true with young children. You are supposed to be guiding and training them. You can't do that if you aren't aware of what they are doing.

If you are in one room and your children are playing in another room, from time to time drift over to the doorway and check out what is going on.

 *Personal Application*

Do you need to supervise more closely? ❑ Yes ❑ No

If you checked "yes," how can you remind yourself to do so?

Use Wisdom about When to Punish

Before you punish your child, take a deep breath and then think it through. There may be more to his or her misbehavior than willful disobedience.

Find out if "disobedience" is caused by a disability.

You may need to take your children in for a physical exam. Following are some disabilities that can underlie what might seem to be disobedience:

- Hearing problem

- Developmental disability

- Learning handicap (such as not being able to remember a sequence of three instructions)

Don't punish for every type of problem.

Evaluate the situation. The following are examples of times that punishment would not be appropriate:

- If a child has an accident, makes a mistake or does something in good faith (such as misunderstanding your instructions and damaging something).

- If a child is tired.

- If a child is sick.

- If a child sucks his or her thumb.

- If a child does not eat enough at meals. (Note, however, that it's wise to withhold dessert in such cases.)

- If a child wets his or her pants when confronted or punished.

- If a child does not fall asleep. (At naptime or nighttime, you can expect your child to quietly stay in bed, but no one can fall asleep with a parent standing over him or her demanding that he or she fall asleep.)

✏ *Personal Application*

Review the above points. Are there times when you should be more understanding instead of punishing?

_____

If you suspect your child is lying:

Dishonesty is rampant in our society. Your children need to learn to tell the truth. If you suspect a child is lying, double check: Call the teacher, a friend's parents, or someone else who may be a reliable source.

If your child has disobeyed and also lied, a double punishment may be appropriate: one punishment for the original misbehavior and one for lying.

If you can't figure out if your child is lying, sometimes it's best to let it go. There will be other times.

However, if your child has a habit of lying, you can punish when you have a 95% certainty. Explain to your child that you need to do this because he or she has developed a bad reputation, but when he or she develops a truthful reputation you will change your approach.

Fantasizing in fun isn't lying.

Personal Application

Do any of your children lie frequently? If so, write a prayer asking for patience and wisdom to deal with this.

Use Short-Term Punishments

Extreme or long-term punishment usually backfires. I have counseled with many adults whose parents were overly strict, sometimes grounding them for long times. These persons developed anger, hurt and resentment.

Short-term punishments usually are most effective.

However, if your child has done something really serious, such as hit a parent, a longer "grounding" and very structured expectations likely are appropriate.

Practice Teamwork

Your children should see you and your spouse as a team. Do not criticize your spouse to your children. Instead, praise your mate and support him or her in front of the kids.

Do not intervene if your spouse disciplines a child.

It is hard to be supportive when you don't like how your spouse is disciplining a child. The desire to intervene may be strong. Yet intervening usually does more harm than good. Your mate becomes upset and your children see you arguing. It usually is better to talk with your spouse later when you are alone.

Another approach would be for you to agree upon a signal either parent could use when concerned about the other's actions. For example, "Could we all take some time-out now?" Then you could have a private talk.

There is an exception to this guideline: If your spouse is physically abusing a child, intervene immediately.

If your spouse berates your children a lot or seems angry much of the time, privately talk with him or her and suggest that you both meet with a biblical counselor. Or ask your pastor for help.

In general, don't overrule your spouse's decisions.

If you disagree with the way your husband or wife handled a situation with the kids, it's usually best not to overturn your mate's decision. Instead, talk privately.

 *Personal Application*

Write any ways in which you have not supported your
spouse in front of the children.

How will you support your mate in the future?

Chapter 5

Use Corporal Punishment Wisely

Brothers, if someone is caught in a sin, you who are spiritual should restore him gently (Galatians 6:1).

Spanking, when done properly, is an effective method to teach children not to engage in inappropriate behavior. Sadly, many people who believe that spanking is okay are cruel and angry when they spank, and they do much harm to their children.

This topic could be a painful one for you if your parents or others abused you when you were a child. It also could be a painful subject if you have seen adults abuse other children.

If you were physically abused as a child, be careful. It is easy to repeat your parents' mistakes. On the other hand, if you were abused, it can be very difficult to discipline your children in any way because of your own painful memories. Determine never to repeat your parents' mistakes, but pray that God will help you not ignore your children's need for discipline because of your past.

Spanking is part of the biblical process.

 He who spares the rod hates his son, but he who loves him is careful to discipline him (Proverbs 13:24).

Folly is bound up in the heart of a child, but the rod of discipline will drive it far from him (Proverbs 22:15).

Do not withhold discipline from a child; if you punish him with the rod, he will not die. Punish him with the rod and save his soul from death (Proverbs 23:13-14)

The rod of correction imparts wisdom, but a child left to himself disgraces his mother (Proverbs 29:15).

Note that "rod" in the previous verses refers to a slender, limber switch. Do not use a belt, electric wire, large piece of wood, or other damaging object when you spank.

Is Spanking Child Abuse?

Some people think that any type of spanking damages children emotionally and constitutes child abuse by definition. This opinion usually is based on a philosophical position or on observations of abusive parents who harm their children physically and emotionally.

Spanking done in love can be effective.

Spanking done by nurturing parents is an entirely different matter. When done with love and self-control, spanking does not teach children to solve problems by fighting, nor does it crush children or destroy their creativity.

Spanking done poorly can wound your children.

If you don't spank properly, you can harm your children emotionally as well as physically. You must discipline in love, not in anger.

Child abuse is real. I have counseled with children who have been severely beaten, who have had broken bones, who have been burned, who have had pins stuck in their arms and who have had their heads placed in a toilet bowl. Any sort of physical mistreatment must not be tolerated.

The following verses show us the importance of having the right attitude and approach when we chastise.

 A man's spirit sustains him in sickness, but a crushed spirit who can bear? (Proverbs 18:14).

Brothers, if someone is caught in a sin, you who are spiritual should restore him gently Galatians 6:1).

Fathers, do not exasperate your children; instead, bring them up in the training and instruction of the Lord (Ephesians 6:4).

Fathers, do not embitter your children, or they will become discouraged (Colossians 3:21).

General Guidelines

How hard should you spank?

Spank hard enough to hurt, but not hard enough to be brutal. Test the force of your spank on yourself. Young children are fragile; be especially careful with them.

At what age should you start spanking?

Don't spank until your child is clearly able to understand, "No." Even then, redirecting a youngster often is the wisest response. Do not spank infants. To some degree, we must "spoil" our babies.

At what age should you stop spanking?

In general, stop at about ten years of age, prior to your child's adolescence. If you follow the guidelines in this book, by the time a child reaches this age, you probably will be spanking him or her rarely since your child will have become obedient and respectful.

Do not spank teenagers. If you do, odds are strong that they will feel humiliated and angry, and that you will do more harm than good.

What are reasons for spanking?

Do not spank your children for every type of misbehavior; if you do, you could fall into the destructive trap of continuously spanking them.

A good beginning place is to target *willful disobedience.* A good first step is to teach the meaning of the word, "No."

Once you establish a basic pattern of obedience, you could also spank for other serious forms of misbehavior such as fighting, blatant disrespect, lying and stealing.

Make sure your requests are clearly understood.

Your children must acknowledge hearing you by saying "yes" or "okay" loudly enough for you to hear. This ensures they heard you and makes it more likely that they will obey you.

It is good to give a brief explanation for your actions. If you only say, "Do not question me," you often will create resentment. However, your children should learn to obey you even when you do not give an explanation.

Punish when children disobey a *first* directive.

As I wrote in the last chapter, you can train your children to respond after you say something one time, or you can train your children to respond after you remind, warn, plead, bribe or threaten. Children learn when their parents mean business.

Typical unhealthy steps that parents take when giving instructions:

- Parent reminds or nags.

- Parent warns or threatens.

- Parent pleads.

- Parent lectures.

- Parent bribes.

- Parent yells.

You may get upset at your children for not responding to your "second chances," but what you are doing is training your children to be disobedient.

You can train your children to respond when you speak quietly or you can train your children to wait until you yell.

Be consistent. If you remind, warn, plead, bribe or threaten, your children will lose respect for you. In addition, you add an unwholesome element of tension into your family.

Your expectations are the key. Your consistent expectation for obedience to your first request, and your predictable actions for disobedience, will be major keys to your success.

 *Personal Application*

Do you violate any of these principles about spanking?
❑ Yes ❑ No

Write any changes you will make if you checked, "Yes."

Follow Ten Steps in Spanking

Following are typical steps in spanking and reconciliation. Be prepared to give the process the time, discussion, thoughtfulness, love and patience it needs. Often, you need to go through all the steps, especially when you are first developing obedience.

With very young children, you can skip some steps.

For example, a simple swat on the rear end following the word "no" may be enough.

1. Prepare yourself spiritually and emotionally.

Check your emotional condition. Are you in control? Are you angry? Pray for God's help, wisdom, strength and love. Never simply react spontaneously.

- Do not spank in anger.

- Take "time-out" to cool off if you need to. Go to your room to settle down. Have your child wait for you in his or her room.

- Remember Scriptures that instruct you to punish in love (Galatians 6:1, Ephesians 6:4 and Colossians 3:21).

2. Evaluate why your child misbehaves.

Sometimes willful disobedience is not the real issue. Ask yourself:

- Is your child reacting to a disability, illness or tiredness?

- Do you reprimand and punish your child in an authoritarian manner instead of a loving manner? If so, you may have set up a "battleground mentality" in your home that actually encourages your child to challenge you.

- Does your child have to misbehave to get your attention? Do you spend loving, accepting, friendly time together?

- Is your child reacting to marital tension or other stresses in your home?

- Is your child reacting to personal problems he or she is facing? For example, if your child is teased all day at school by other children, he or she may come home frustrated and ready to misbehave.

- Is your child reacting to hidden guilt? Are there other issues to which you should be sensitive?

- Does your child think he or she is "bad" or "evil" and act out to be punished?

- If there has been a divorce, is your child feeling responsible and acting out to be punished?

- Is your child confused or unable to do what you asked? (Some children, for example, can only remember one thing you tell them to do, not three things.)

After you ask yourself the above questions, you may decide you should not spank your child. It's also possible you will decide that a spanking is needed, even if the answer to one of these questions is, "Yes." However, you will have greater understanding and will be more aware of issues to discuss with your child.

3. Meet with your child in a private place.

This removes embarrassment for your child, or the need to perform before an audience (such as brothers, sisters or friends).

If the misbehavior takes place in a public place, take your child to a private location before disciplining.

4. Have a two-way discussion. Don't give a speech!

Getting your child involved in the discussion is much more effective than giving a speech.

If your child is loud or boisterous, have him or her go to the bedroom or a quiet place to wait until he or she is ready to talk. Do not engage in a wild argument.

Watch your words and your tone of voice.

- Give the emotional message of loving concern, not hate. Remember, you are your child's friend.

- Do not express disgust or call your child names. Do not give the message that your child is "bad" in a unique way. Rather, give the message that what he or she did is wrong. Remember, you are training, not simply punishing.

- Act serious. Show concern about the situation.

- Sometimes it is good to express sorrow, grief, personal disappointment or anger.

  - It is good for your child to experience guilt for serious misbehavior.

  - Do not overdo it. You do not want to "break your child's spirit."

  - Do not approach your child this way too often. It will lose its impact.

- Talk in a quiet tone of voice most of the time.

- Do not say, "This hurts me more than it hurts you." You may think this is true, but it sounds silly to your child.

- Be careful not to overdo statements such as, "You really hurt God," "You sinned against God" or "You can't go to Heaven if you do that." You can drive your child away from God.

Clarify what your child did wrong.

- It's usually better not to ask, "Did you…?" This sets the stage for lying and just gives you one more issue to deal with. Instead, say something such as, "We need to talk about your disobeying me when I told you to …"

- Usually, do not ask, "Why?" with very young children. The only real answer often is, "Because I wanted to." There are exceptions. At times it may be appropriate to ask, "Why?" (For example, "Why did you hit your brother?")

Help your child learn to accept responsibility.

- Who's feeling the anxiety? Children sometimes put parents on the defensive about their actions or the rules. Focus the discussion back on your child's actions.

- When a child learns to develop sorrow, not anger, he or she is developing a conscience.

- If your child says that spanking is not justified, allow a brief discussion.

  - There may be facts you should know.

  - Listen carefully, and then make up your mind. Do not engage in a debate, or think that your child must agree that he or she should be spanked. (Some parents who feel guilty about spanking almost plead with their children to agree it is okay.)

Help your child learn from the situation.

Have your child think of and then discuss alternatives to the misbehavior. Help him or her learn from the incident. Ask, "How else could you have handled this?"

- This is hard for children.

- Be careful not to lecture or do all the work. Your goal is for your child to think of alternatives.

- If your child can't think of alternatives right away, you could have him or her sit on a chair or their bed until they can come up with alternatives.

5. Spank your child.

- Have a routine position for your child to assume. Train your child to remain in that position.

- Use a switch or similar thin object. Do not use a belt, electric wire, large piece of wood, or anything else that can damage your child.

- Spank the child's seat. Never slap, hit, or poke the head, legs, arm, back or other parts of the body.

- Allow your child to leave his or her underpants on. Do not humiliate your child.

- Make sure it hurts, but do not be brutal.

  - Do not spank so softly that your child feels nothing.

  - And do not overdo it! Children are fragile. Remember, do not spank in anger.

  - Test the force of the spanking on yourself.

6. Expect your child needs to respond appropriately.

- Train your child to say, "I'm sorry" and show repentance.

- Crying often is appropriate in younger children (but not screams of rage). Do not insist that your child cry.

Treat it as a second incident if your child responds inappropriately to your spanking by rolling his or her eyes, whining, sassing, arguing, pouting, throwing tantrums, screaming in rage, wiggling, wrestling or hitting you. Do not accept it as "okay" or a normal part of your family life for your child to respond inappropriately.

If your child responds inappropriately:

- Ask yourself:

  - Are you practicing the positive parenting practices discussed in the previous chapters?

  - Did you follow the above steps in spanking and reconciliation? Go over each point and evaluate yourself.

  - Did you spank too hard, or in anger?

  - Did you spank too softly?

- Start all over again and go through the ten steps, this time focusing on your child's inappropriate reaction.

  - Although a second spanking may be appropriate, be careful not to get into the trap of having ongoing spanking after spanking. "Time-out," spending time in the bedroom or extra chores may be more effective consequences and can prevent the potential trap of ongoing spankings. They also can help you avoid getting into power struggles with your child.

  - Sometimes it's best to wait until the tension level drops before administering a second punishment. Have your child wait in his or her room until he or she is ready to talk.

- Later, after everything is over, talk with your child about his or her inappropriate reaction and agree on plans for changes in the future. Be sure that the groundwork is laid for appropriate reactions in future situations. Make sure your child knows this is something that is serious and that it must change. Practicing ("role-playing") appropriate responses may be helpful.

7. Pray with your child.

Train your child to pray, out loud, following these steps:

- Tell God he or she is sorry for the specific misbehavior.

- Ask God for forgiveness.

- Ask for help to do better with this problem in the future.

Pray for your child to do better and thank God for forgiving him or her.

Help your child understand God's forgiveness if he or she seems crushed. Your child needs to accept and experience forgiveness, not live with guilt. Sensitive children need to learn that of course they make mistakes. It isn't the end of the world. For some children, it may be helpful to share the following:

- Christian growth is progressive. None of us is perfect (Philippians 3:12). Many great people in the Bible can be seen to be imperfect.

- When we sin and ask for forgiveness, God forgives us (1 John 1:9).

- The father forgave his prodigal son and was delighted to see his repentance (Luke 15:11-32).

- Once we pray, we need to press on (Philippians 3:12-14).

8. Reconcile with your child.

- Tell your child you forgive him or her.

- Tell your child you love him or her.

- Hug your child.

9. Have your child practice restitution.

Your child should apologize to anyone else he or she has wronged and ask forgiveness. It may be appropriate for your child to hug the other person.

Train your child to forgive any others who also were involved.

Your child should take care of any damage he or she caused.

- Examples:

    - Clean up a mess.

    - Pay for a broken window.

    - Do extra chores to "pay" for damages.

- Do not overdo this (for example, by assigning a child three months of extra chores).

10. After the event, treat it as over.

Do not keep bringing it up. Return to your normal, friendly interactions.

 *Personal Application*

Changes I need to make in the way I spank my children:

One More Suggestion

Don't make major changes in your approach until you read Chapters 6 and 7. Chapter 6 covers the importance of teaching as well various other consequences. Chapter 7 describes how to set up a family meeting to explain the changes.

Chapter 6
Use Other Consequences

Listen, my son, to your father's instruction and do not forsake your mother's teaching (Proverbs 1:8).

Spanking is only one tool parents have. In this chapter, we will take a look at several other tools, ranging from teaching techniques to alternative types of punishment. As you read this chapter, remember the guidelines about parental authority in Chapter 4.

Teach Your Children

Before studying more about punishment, let's look at the importance of teaching our children *how* to live their lives. We should teach them what to do, not simply what they should not do. Although punishment sometimes is appropriate, it should not be your primary teaching tool. Children need training and instruction (teaching).

 Fathers, do not exasperate your children; instead, bring them up in the training and instruction of the Lord (Ephesians 6:4).

Many parents assume a child is being disobedient when, in fact, the child is doing his or her best. Do not assume that your child knows how to do something until you're sure you have taught him or her.

Both parents are responsible to teach.

 Listen, my son, to your father's instruction and do not forsake your mother's teaching (Proverbs 1:8).

Also study Deuteronomy 6:6-9; Deuteronomy 11:18-21; Proverbs 4:1-5 and Proverbs 6:20.

 *Personal Application*

Do you teach your children *how* to do things, or simply tell them to do things?

Use these teaching strategies.
There are lots of ways to teach. Some of them:

- **Praise.**
  Catch your children being good. Look for good things they do and comment on them!

- **Encourage.**
  We all can feel overwhelmed or unappreciated. Everyone needs encouragement, including your children.

- **Give rewards.**
  Giving rewards, particularly to young children, can help establish appropriate behaviors.
  Reward for doing something positive, not just for staying out of trouble. For example, if Joe frequently squabbles with his brother, Tom, do not reward Joe for simply staying out of trouble with Tom. Instead, reward him for helping Tom, praising Tom, playing cooperatively with Tom or ignoring Tom's provocative comments. In this way, you will help Joe practice doing positive things with Tom instead of just staying away from Tom.
  Reward, do not bribe. A reward system is a purposeful, thought-out system that you set up to help your children develop new habits. A bribe is when a child threatens you with bad behavior unless you pay him or her off, or when you keep offering to give your child something to get him or her to behave.
  Reward improvements. Do not wait for perfection.
  Keep records. It can be helpful if you keep records on charts that your child can see.

- **Ask your child how he or she wants to change.**

    When someone says that he or she wants to improve in a specific area, the person usually is more willing to work at making the changes.

- **Offer to work together on a mutual problem.**

    If both you and a child have an anger problem, offer to go through an anger workbook together.

- **Tell stories to young children.**

    Inventing your own stories with moral lessons imbedded in them can be fun and an effective way to teach.

- **Role-play.**

    Have your children practice appropriate behavior.

 *Personal Application*

Teaching strategies that I plan to use:

More Consequences

Following are various responses you may want to consider when your children misbehave.

Redirect young children.
Redirecting a child's attention, rather than punishment, is often appropriate for very young children.

Assign "time-out" for short periods of time.
Here are three ideas for using time-out.

- Have your child take time-out for a few quiet minutes sitting on a chair.

- Give a "rebate" for taking time-out appropriately. For example:

  - Place your child on time-out for six minutes.

  - If he or she takes it perfectly (no talking, kicking, etc.), after three minutes you announce that a three-minute rebate has been earned and that time-out is over.

- Place a child on "time-out" for an indefinite period of time—until your child comes out of his or her room with a good attitude and apologizes. The length of time, therefore, is up to him or her.

Assign extra chores.
Extra chores for 10 or 15 minutes can be very effective with teenagers.

Take away specific privileges for a period of time.
Be careful about this. Do not make a child's life too grim by restricting him or her from everything and everybody or you will bring about resentment or rebellion.

"Ground" your child for a relatively short time.

Have your child pay restitution.
If a child stole something, damaged someone else's property or hurt someone, he or she needs to apologize to the other person(s) and make restitution.

Assign extra schoolwork for missed assignments.

With teenagers, have a simple two-way talk
Punishment may not be necessary.

Don't take away something a child earned.
It's usually a bad idea to punish your child by taking away a reward you previously gave him or her. It is important to follow through on previous promises unless it seems absolutely necessary to change them.

Assign "slave time" for tardiness to church
Skeeter and I noticed that our children often were not ready for church on time, so we set up a system in which those who were ready would earn "slave time" from those who were not ready.

The system:

- Everyone (including Skeeter and me) had to be sitting on the couch at 8:30 a.m., ready for church. Before saying we were ready, we had to make our bed, eat cereal and fruit, take a vitamin pill, brush our teeth, dress and then get our Bible, coat and anything we planned to take to church.

- Each person who was one to four minutes late owed five minutes of slave time to those who were ready.

- Each person who was five to nine minutes late owed ten minutes of slave time to those who were ready.

- Each person who was ten to fourteen minutes late owed fifteen minutes of slave time to those who were ready.

The results: Our boys quickly developed the habit of getting ready for church on time. Skeeter and I, however, did not do nearly so well, and ended up putting in a lot of slave time for the boys!

 *Personal Application*

Which of these alternative consequences will you try?

Chapter 7
Talk Before Changing How You Discipline

The wise in heart are called discerning, and pleasant
words promote instruction (Proverbs 16:21).

In this chapter, you will learn how to prepare your children for changes in your expectations and disciplinary procedures.

Meet with Your Spouse

Have a pre-meeting with your mate before talking with the children. If you are a single parent, it may be helpful to meet with a mature Christian friend of the same sex who has seen you interact with your children and who would be willing to offer you feedback about what he or she has seen.

When you and your spouse (or friend) talk, discuss changes you need to make in:

- Centering your family in Christ.

- Creating a more nurturing home.

- Expecting obedience (for example, expecting your children to obey when you say something one time, quietly).

- Disciplining consistently and lovingly.

Try to agree about changes you need to make. Take as much time to talk as you need. Learn from each other. Compromise if necessary. Do your best to present a united approach.

If you are a stepparent:
If you are a stepparent, beware of trying to "shape the kids up" when you marry someone who already has children. First work on developing a relationship with the children. Review Chapter 3.

If your spouse is uninvolved:
If your spouse is removed, refusing to be involved in teaching or discipline, or if he or she frequently criticizes your ideas or actions, try to get him or her involved by:

- Asking for advice. Be sure to respond to it respectfully.

- Asking him or her to take care of a situation. Do nothing yourself. Say that you will follow your spouse's lead.

- Asking if you have been too assertive or controlling and have not given him or her a chance to be heard.

If your spouse won't get involved, you may have to ask him or her to support you and then do the best you can alone.

If your spouse strongly opposes spanking (or discipline of any type) or opposes you in front of the kids, it may be best not to do anything now. When your children misbehave, it may be wisest to back off and tell your spouse that you will let him or her deal with the problem.

Hold a Family Meeting

Both parents should be present. A single parent can ask a family friend to help talk with the children if he or she feels the need for support. However, he or she must be ready to take the role of an authority figure with her children after the meeting.

Approach your children as a team.

Do not just "lower the boom." Allow open discussion. Be friendly. Although you need to be friendly, also be authoritative. You are not pleading for your children's understanding or agreement. You will not take a vote on most issues.

Step-By-Step Meeting Guide

Pray.

Ask for God's direction and blessing on the meeting.

Read and discuss Scriptures.

Study the following verses that illustrate your responsibilities and your children's responsibilities. (Many are written out in Chapter 4.)

- **Your responsibilities:**

  - To discipline (Proverbs 19:18).

  - To discipline and spank (Proverbs 13:24, 22:15, 23:13-14 and 29:15).

- **Your children's responsibilities:**

  - To honor (respect) (Exodus 20:12; Deuteronomy 5:16; Ephesians 6:2-3).

  - To obey (Ephesians 6:1; Colossians 3:20).

  - To learn (Proverbs 4:1-5 and 13:1).

Review your family's current practices.

Review things as you see them. Then ask your children's opinions about things they'd like to change in your family.

Although you know that certain changes will be made, be open to your children's comments or observations. Be ready to use good ideas. This will help them feel more involved in the process.

Apologize if you have not shown respect in the past (for example, by calling them names) or have been unloving or unwise in your disciplinary procedures. Ask their forgiveness.

Shown that you are ready to change yourself. Seeing that you are ready to change will help your children be ready to change.

Go over your new expectations.

Let them know you will give instructions lovingly and quietly.

Then say that when you tell them to do something you expect them to say, "Yes" or "okay." Add that you expect them to obey right away without reminders.

Review how your children can politely question or protest your instructions, and their responsibility to accept your final decision.

Discuss your new discipline procedures.

These will be what you and your spouse decided on in your pre-meeting.

Practice ("role-play") your new procedures.

Make it fun. Take turns playing the roles of parent and child. Things that you can role-play:

- The wrong ways things are done now. Include things your children do wrong when you give a directive and things you do wrong (such as nagging and pleading).

- The proper way to say "okay" and follow instructions.

- Spanking procedures that will be followed for disobedience.

Announce a future family meeting.

Plan another meeting in one week to review how things are going.

Pray.

Ask each person to take turns praying, asking for God's help for his or her part. Wrap things up with an over-all prayer by a parent.

After the Family Meeting

Be sure that your over-all family interactions are positive. Review the material on making God the center of your home and nurturing to be sure that your actions are friendly, respectful and balanced.

Be ready to be tested.

Be consistent in your expectations.

Do not warn, remind, nag, plead or threaten.

Be patient.

Do not try to change everything at once! Prioritize obedience. Some changes will take time. Watch your frustration. Show your love.

Praise improvements.

Do not wait for perfection to give out some positives.

Go over this book frequently.

Review key guidelines to be sure you do forget any important points.

Daily review with your mate how things are going.

Husband and wife should talk privately every night to review how they are doing. Approach these meetings in a spirit of teamwork, as two persons trying to learn how to do it right. Start each meeting with prayer. Single parents can ask their friends to watch and comment on how they interact with their children.

Do not lower your standards when things improve.

Once things get better, it's common for people to lower their expectations and start to let things slide. Then before they know it, they are back to the bad old days.

Hold a follow-up family meeting.

Get together in one week. Review good events as well as problems. Ask if anyone has suggestions.

Personal Application

Write your plans to have a family meeting and make changes. When will you meet? What will the changes be?

Part III:
Create a Climate of Growth

8. Cultivate Character Development

9. Encourage Responsible Behavior

10. Develop Each Child's Talents and Intellect

11. Prepare for Marriage and Sex

12. Change Approaches with Teenagers

Chapter 8
Cultivate Character Development

*But the fruit of the Spirit is love, joy, peace, patience,
kindness, goodness, faithfulness, gentleness
and self-control (Galatians 5:22-23).*

As your children grow up—and when they leave home—
they will be exposed to major societal and cultural pressures
that conflict with Christian values.

We, as well as our children, are more influenced by our
culture than we realize. We embrace the world's propaganda
and become ineffective as God's ambassadors. We accept lies
and compromise our witness without knowing it. We try to fit
into our culture instead of invading our culture.

Emphasize true values.

It's easy to focus on our children's grades, athletic ability,
beauty, intelligence or popularity. Although these have a
place in life, they should not be most important to us. Instead,
we primarily should be concerned about what type of people
our children are becoming.

You can help your children rise above your culture's in-
fluences by emphasizing God's true values. Recognize
achievements, but emphasize what's most important.

I remember a struggle I went through along these lines as
our children were growing up. I wanted them to succeed at
school, so I'd look for good grades on their report cards.

But I knew that grades, although important, were not as important as their teachers' comments about their character. So when I reviewed a report card, I made myself focus first on the teacher's comments. If a teacher wrote that one of my sons was kind, generous or helpful, I made sure I praised my son for that before commenting on his grades.

Paul wrote about true values when he discussed the fruit of the Spirit. Let's take a look at what he said:

 But the fruit of the Spirit is love, joy, peace, patience, kindness, goodness, faithfulness, gentleness and self-control (Galatians 5:22-23).

Encourage your children to grow the fruit of the Spirit. Some ways you could do this would be to praise them when they:

✓ Reach out to others

✓ Share

✓ Exercise positive leadership

✓ Demonstrate good sportsmanship

 *Personal Application*

Think back over the last two weeks. What have you emphasized or commented on the most regarding your children's performance or character?

Help your children break free from cultural lies.

It's hard not to be influenced by ungodly voices in our culture, since they are always around us. To help your children break free, help them realize that their citizenship is in heaven, and that God's values and truths are all that matter.

 Do not conform any longer to the pattern of this world, but be transformed by the renewing of your mind. Then you will be able to test and approve what God's will is—his good, pleasing and perfect will (Romans 12:2).

Dear friends, I urge you, as aliens and strangers in the world, to abstain from sinful desires, which war against your soul (1 Peter 2:11).

The world and its desires pass away, but the man who does the will of God lives forever (1 John 2:17).

Train Your Children as Missionaries

I sometimes counsel with Christian teenagers who are in secular high schools. For many high schoolers, these are awkward and lonely years. Christian teens sometimes feel even more isolated and alienated, since Christianity often is not valued by most of the other kids or teachers.

Christian teenagers in this situation often hide their faith. Some are embarrassed to be Christians and do not reach out to others. For them, high school is a time of survival, of hiding their Christianity while avoiding getting caught up in too many bad things. Often the end result is that their faith slips, and they become increasingly influenced by the other kids.

Encourage your children to be influencers.

Help your children see themselves as ambassadors of Christ (2 Corinthians 5:20), people who have something to offer. We are to be lights shining like stars in the world (Philippians 2:15).

Encourage teenagers (and adults) to take a stand, to reach out—to have the attitude, "I'm going to make a difference." Why? *Because either we are going to influence other people, or they are going to influence us.* When our children develop this attitude, it is the perfect antidote to peer pressure.

We need not be obnoxious about our faith, hitting people on the head with our Bibles. Yet we need to be praying for them and looking for opportunities to share the Word of life. If I want to overcome the temptations offered by others, I need to say, "I'm going to reach out to others and minister to them."

Study Scriptures with your children which illustrate the importance of reaching out, of being missionaries to those around us.

 We are therefore Christ's ambassadors, as though God were making his appeal through us (2 Corinthians 5:20).

Each of you should look not only to your own interests, but also to the interests of others (Philippians 2:3-4).

Witness to others yourself.

You will be a living example as your children watch and listen to you share Christ with others.

When you talk about non-Christians, emphasize their need for salvation.

Invite non-Christians to dinner.

Pray as a family ahead of time. Ask God to save them, to help your family be a good witness and to give you an opportunity to share the Word.

After they leave, pray as a family for their salvation.

Pray with your children for their friends.

Have a "Faith Club" at your home.

 *Personal Application*

My plans to train my children to approach others as a missionary:

Help Your Children Become Friends

Sibling rivalry is real, it is common and it is found in the Scriptures.

✓ Cain killed Abel (Genesis 4:3-8).

✓ Jacob made Esau give him his birthright before he gave him food (Genesis 25:29 32). Then he stole Esau's blessing (Genesis 27:1-41).

✓ Most of Joseph's brothers wanted to kill him (Genesis 37:1-20).

✓ Jesus' family mocked his ministry (Mark 3:31-35).

Happily, the Bible also has some examples of close siblings.

✓ Andrew told Simon Peter about Jesus (John 1:40-42).

✓ Reuben loved Joseph (Genesis 37:21-22).

 *Personal Application*

I see sibling rivalry between my children.
❑ Yes ❑ No

Describe their problems:

Make a strategy to overcome sibling rivalry.

Some people say, "Sibling rivalry is normal. There's nothing you can do about it. Let them work it out themselves. When they grow up, they will become friends."

This is not wise. Children learn the "law of the jungle" and miss out on the joy of developing close bonds.

You are responsible to teach your children how to become close friends. Do not let things "take their course" naturally. Make it your goal for your children to be good friends.

Teach your children to encourage each other.

Have your children praise, support and help each other. For example, have an older child go to his or her sibling's open house at school to look at and compliment the brother or sister's projects.

This approach helps older siblings learn how to deal with younger ones (who may seem childish, irritating or embarrassing).

Do not allow tattling.

Tattling is not helping. Parents are responsible to supervise. Do not put your children in a supervisory position if possible.

"Helpful tattling" is only appropriate for major events or concerns.

But encourage your children to report on positive things their siblings did.

Have children pray for one another.

Teach them how to ask and grant forgiveness.

Play games as a family.

Develop the sense of a "family team."

Teach good sportsmanship.

Have them play together (not spending much time in front of TV). Play with them; be an example sharing and how to lose or win graciously

Watch out for parental favoritism.

- Scriptural examples:

    - Isaac-Esau and Rebecca-Jacob (Genesis 25:28).

    - Israel-Joseph (Genesis 37:3).

- Do not compare children one to another.

- Do not build one child up significantly more than others.

- Usually, do not criticize or punish one child in the presence of his or her brothers or sisters.

- Do not overemphasize one child's good looks.

- Do not give all special lessons or opportunities to the most "gifted" child.

- Be aware. You may be neglecting a child.

Do not always try to be absolutely "fair."

Although, it's good to be fair in general, don't spend time trying to be absolutely fair over picky little things (such as weighing desserts to be sure each child gets exactly the same amount).

Eat meals as a family.

Go on family camping trips.

Be sensitive when a new baby enters the home.

Be sure to give attention to the children who already are there.

Protect younger children.

Do not allow older children to take advantage of younger ones. For example, do not let younger kids do older kids' chores.

Have your kids baby-sit themselves as a team.

When your children are old enough to be left without a baby-sitter, instead of leaving one absolutely in charge, you could have each responsible for the other, and each earning baby-sitting pay. The oldest would have the final authority if there were any disagreements that couldn't be mutually agreed upon, but each of the younger children would have the authority to talk to you when you come home if he or she felt there had been an abuse of power.

Allow older children to have friends of their own.

Help brothers and sisters deal with jealousy.

Do not allow teasing.

Deal with fighting.

Help them learn how to resolve problems themselves. There are three phases to this process.

- **Phase one.** The training phase. This may take many months.

  - Let children know that fighting is not tolerated.

  - Discover the truth. Often, sending them to separate rooms and speaking to them individually is the best idea.

- If each child did something wrong, punish both, each for his or her part. (Although the punishment should vary depending on what each child did, and on their respective ages, each child may have contributed to the problem.)

- Do not say, "You do not love your brother/sister."

- Teach problem-solving skills. Help them talk about alternatives.

- Help them identify recurring patterns.

- Reconciliation afterwards is important. Have them hug and forgive each other.

- **Phase two.** Again, this may take many months. As your children grow older and demonstrate the ability to intelligently discuss their fights:

  - Have them retire to a separate room, talk and agree on a proposed resolution.

  - Have them report back to you with their proposed solution. When they report back, make sure the solution has not been forced upon one by the other. It must be fair to both and reasonable.

- **Phase three.** When your children consistently have shown the ability to come up with good solutions, ask them to work things out without reporting back (although they can ask for help). From time to time, however, ask how they have been resolving problems.

Help older children deal with younger children.

It's common for an older child to feel irritated by a younger sibling. One typical problem is when the older child and a friend want to play alone, and the younger sibling feels left out.

Your task is to help each of them understand the other one's feelings. The younger child must learn to allow the older one to have time with his or her friend and the older child needs to make special time for the younger one another time.

 *Personal Application*

My plans to help my children become close friends:

Teach How to Act with Adults

Train children when they are young in basic social graces with adults. Examples include shaking hands, hugging relatives and saying, "Thank you."

Chapter 9

Encourage
Responsible Behavior

A wise son brings joy to his father, but a foolish son grief to his mother (Proverbs 10:1).

Developing responsibility is a *process* that starts when children are young and continues throughout all their years at home. With very young children, you have a structured, parent-controlled environment. As your children get older, slowly change your parenting style, transferring more responsibility to them. Your goal is for your children to learn how to act responsibly when they are not with you.

Let Children Make Choices

Rules and standards are necessary, especially with younger children as you lay a foundation for their lives. Examples of our rules:

- TV was limited to one hour on days preceding school days (usually Sunday through Thursday) and two hours on Fridays, Saturdays and holidays. They were prohibited from watching shows we felt would be bad for them.

- When in the car, they had to sit politely. Joking was okay, but not poking, pushing or loud conversation.

Routines such as making the bed and brushing teeth also are important.

Offer more choices as children grow older.

Give them opportunities to make decisions or to share in the decision-making process. Your rules, alone, won't prepare your children for adulthood.

This is an ongoing and changing process.

- Very young children have few choices.

- As our children grow older, we need to identify areas in which we feel comfortable giving them more choices.

- Of course, we need to talk with them and help them learn how to make good choices.

- I would rather have my children stumble and fall when at home and I'm available to help, than make them wait until they leave home before they have an opportunity to stumble.

- The goal is to say "no" rarely in the months just before your children leave home. However, you do need to be willing to say "no" when necessary. You are going through a training process, not suddenly granting complete freedom.

If you give a choice, be sure it is a real choice. Do not offer a choice, then take it away because a child made the wrong choice.

Examples of areas of possible choices.

- What your children wear to school. (Idea: Allow them to purchase their own clothes with a clothing allowance.)

- Activities in which your children can participate.

 *Personal Application*

What are some choices you would feel comfortable giving your children this week?

_____

Have children plan their activities.

If your children say, "I'm bored. There's nothing to do," share various activity ideas with them, but then give them the responsibility to make choices or think of new projects. Do not assume the responsibility to entertain them all the time.

Have Your Children Do Chores

Children need to learn how do things, not simply be taken care of. Yet it can be frustrating teaching them how to do chores. At first, you can do them in less time than it takes to show your children how to do them, but your children need the training. Do not say, "Get out of the way. I can do it better."

Examples of chores
We expected our boys to keep their bedrooms clean and also do daily chores such as cleaning the dishes and feeding the dog. On Saturdays we had them do two to three hours regular Saturday chores. A few times a year, we had Saturday workdays for everyone.

Let your children help choose chores.
You could have periodic family meetings during which your children could participate, choosing chores they prefer.

Work with your children.
When you work on major chores with your children, you have an opportunity to get closer to them. Plus, they can learn from your industrious example. One other benefit: If they see you working beside them, they are less likely to feel like slaves.

Don't nag. Use time limits instead.
Parents tend to nag children about doing their chores. Try this method as a way to avoid nagging:

If a child has responsibilities such as getting ready for school, cleaning a bedroom or doing chores, set a time by which the task must be done. Do not remind or nag your child to complete the project. Wait until the time is up, then reward your child with praise or credit toward his or her allowance. If the chore hasn't been completed, require your child to finish it (with no allowance credit) before having free time. In addition, add a 10 to 15 minutes penalty chore.

 *Personal Application*

Write any changes you need to make in your family's chore systems.

Train Children to Manage Money

Many children leave home unprepared to deal with budgeting or handling money. Some suggestions to help get them started on the right foot:

- Consider giving them a small allowance with which they can buy small items.

- Consider paying them to do chores so they can earn money for larger purchases.

- Consider giving older children clothing money and giving them the authority to buy their own clothes.

- Teach them to tithe and be prepared to give offerings to for special needs.

- Teach them to save.

- Train older children how to open a bank account and balance a checkbook.

- Thoroughly show them the danger of buying things on credit.

 *Personal Application*

How will you train your children to be wise with money?

Do Not Be Overprotective

Some parents are so aware of potential dangers facing their children that they are overprotective and keep their children from doing anything with the slightest degree of risk. We need to monitor our children's activities and teach them appropriate caution, but we do not want them to turn into fearful recluses.

Encourage Christian Friendships

The people we spend time with affect us. The same is true of your children. Help them identify sincere Christian friends who can encourage them in their faith. One way to do this is to make friends with people who have children of the same age, then get together as families.

Chapter 10
Develop Each Child's Talents and Intellect

Now the body is not made up of one part but of many (1 Corinthians 12:14).

Encourage Skill Development

God created each of us with different abilities, skills and interests. Provide your children with a variety of experiences to give them exposure to different activities. For example, over the years sign them up for swimming and tennis lessons, a painting class and soccer practice. Ask them to help you cook, garden and change a tire on the car. Take them to your place of work and show them what you do.

As your children grow older, help them identify their abilities, interests and skills. Then help them develop these areas. But don't overdo the activities. Family time is important. And remember, growing the fruit of the Spirit (review Chapter 8) is their most important task.

Personal Application

My plans to encourage my children's skill development:

Encourage Intellectual Development

Continually provide a rich variety of experiences at home and away from home. Make these fun activities. Don't try to force intellectual or physical skills too early.

The following are several things you can do to help your children develop their intellect.

Babies

Dangle interesting things over their crib (such as an enlarged photo of your face). Have posters and a safe mirror near the crib.

Give them safe space to roam, lots of safe objects to grab, their own cupboard in the kitchen and toys for the bathtub.

Interact with them. Sing to them, talk to them, tickle and gently bounce them.

Preschoolers

Provide simple things to encourage creativity, such as art supplies (paste, papers, crayons and scissors), musical instruments, sewing supplies, wood working supplies, shovels and bare ground.

Expensive, fancy toys often aren't the best choice. Instead, choose toys that encourage creativity and thought. For example, wooden blocks and big cardboard blocks.

Take your children to the library. Read to them every day.

Limit TV, perhaps to one hour per day on school days and two hours on holidays or weekends. Monitor what they watch.

Take field trips. Even a trip to the grocery store can be a field trip. Also go camping, to an almond factory or to a bread bakery.

Play board games.

Give your children Proverbs to chew on.

School-age children

As your children grow older, let them use a camera, teach them games you played as a child, teach them songs and acquire pets. Take them to the tops of mountains, the desert and the beach. Keep reading aloud.

Expose your children to other cultures. Consider housing a foreign student, or sending your teenage children abroad for a summer.

Involve your children in what you do: Church activities, picketing abortion clinics, visiting nursing homes, cooking and gardening.

Let your children spend some time with you on the job.

Personal Application

My plans to encourage my children's intellectual development:

_____

Create a "Livable" Home

Allow your children to play creatively. Make sure parts of your home and yard are open for them to make tents, build walls with blocks and explore with other toys.

If you have young children, put precious ceramics, dangerous cleaning supplies and medicines out of reach. This will protect your children and remove the need for you to frequently say, "No."

Allow a reasonable activity level.

Your children need to learn good manners, but do not expect them to just quietly sit around.

Personal Application

Where can your children play creatively in your home?

Write your plans if you need to designate a play area for them.

Identify Educational Goals

One of your children's tasks is to learn as much as they can to prepare for their future. Encourage them to do well at their studies.

 Whatever you do, work at it with all your heart, as working for the Lord, not for men (Colossians 3:23).

Some think education and college are bad. Others think straight A's and a college education are a necessity. Neither extreme is necessarily right. The key is to identify your child's talents and abilities, and seek God for the path he would want them to take.

Decide who will teach your children.

There are many choices: public school, home school, Christian school or non-Christian private school. This is an individual choice. There is no "correct" Christian decision.

Don't allow yourself to be pressured to make one choice or another. And don't feel guilty if you make a different decision next year.

Work with the School

If your child goes to school, involve yourself with the school. You have a partnership with the staff and teachers. Together you are trying to provide your child with the best possible educational experience.

Get involved.

It's nice if you can be a classroom aide or help in other ways that involve your presence with the children.

If a child has problems, talk with the teacher.

Daily or weekly written reports sometimes are useful.

If teacher-child problems come up, be open minded.

Do not automatically side with child or teacher. Be especially careful not to automatically assume the teacher is being mean or unfair.

If you disagree with a teacher, do so respectfully.

Express respect and let him or her know you want to work together. Don't be hostile. If you can't come to an agreement over curriculum, activities or books, be prepared to take a stand, but do so politely.

If you think your child has a bad teacher, or the teacher has a personality conflict with your child, try to help your child deal with the situation. If that doesn't work, and communicating with the teacher doesn't help, ask the principal to help. Remember to approach all meetings with an open mind and cooperative spirit. You'll usually get much farther than if you are hostile or aggressive.

 *Personal Application*

Write any changes you need to make in your relationship with the school.

Teach Respect for Teachers

Teach your children to respect and (usually) obey teachers (Romans 13:1). Be respectful when you talk with your children about a teacher or school administrators.

Let your children know teachers may be wrong.

Children can look upon teachers as ultimate authorities. Let them know that the Bible is our ultimate authority.

Say that a teacher may need salvation.

With older children, pray together for the teacher.

 *Personal Application*

Do you need to give your child a different message about his or her teachers? ❏ Yes ❏ No

If you checked "yes," what changes should you make?

Prepare for Public School Issues

If your child will attend public school, before the school year starts, prepare him or her for issues that may come up. Although you can't be an expert on everything, be ready to talk about common issues such as:

✓ Evolution

✓ Dinosaurs

✓ Halloween celebrations

✓ Sex education

✓ Relativism

✓ Homosexuality

✓ Bible as a "myth"

✓ Direct misrepresentation of Christianity

✓ Indirect put-downs of Christianity

✓ Humanism

✓ Political viewpoints

Teach your children to be "polite rebels."

If your children are in public school, let them know they must respect their teachers, but it's okay to disagree courteously. Help them feel comfortable basing their opinions on the Bible.

Help with Homework

Good study habits are helpful to learning academic subjects. They also provide training in responsibility, commitment and self-control.

Stay aware of your children's homework. Let them know you are interested and proud of their accomplishments. Praise and encouragement are important. Do not fall into the nagging trap.

If a child doesn't do homework, try to find out why. Set up study times and systems as needed, with a rule that there is no free time until homework is completed.

 *Personal Application*

Do you need to help your children more with their homework? ❏ Yes ❏ No

If so, what steps should you take?

Respond to Grades with Wisdom

As I wrote in Chapter 8, emphasize citizenship grades. Of course, also pay attention to academic grades.

Praise success.

Be careful not to always focus on grades that could be improved. It is easy to continually "up the ante" and give children the message that what they do never is good enough.

Be aware of your children's abilities.

Do not press your children to achieve beyond what they are able. On the other hand, encourage a child if he or she is an underachiever.

Be Balanced Home School Parents

I have a deep respect for parents who home school their children. Most of those I know do a great job giving their children a good education, teaching them God's ways, developing the fruit of the Spirit and exposing them to other children. However, here are a few suggestions based on observations I've made over the years:

Neither parent should make the other home school.

From time to time, a husband pressures his wife to home school their children even though she doesn't share his passion. Since this would be such a tremendous commitment for her, she should be in agreement with the plan before starting.

Home school parents shouldn't neglect their mate.

If you are a home school parent, remember that your primary responsibility is to your spouse. You are one flesh and are called to cleave together. Prioritize this primary relationship and set aside enough time for it to blossom. Spend time talking each day. Take walks together. Go on dates. Don't reject God's design. Review Chapter 3 for more ideas.

A parent should feel free to stop home schooling.

Some parents decide to discontinue home schooling. Perhaps their life circumstances have changed. Or perhaps they have discovered they weren't as effective as they hoped. Or perhaps their child has requested to go to school and they have decided to honor their child's request.

These parents often feel like failures, sometimes because other home school parents criticize them. That's regrettable.

If you decide to stop home schooling and others condemn you, reject their messages. Read how Paul responded to unwise criticism in 1 Corinthians 4:3-4. He was concerned about what God thought, not others who condemned him.

Chapter 11

Prepare for Marriage and Sex

*For this reason a man will leave his father and mother
and be united to his wife, and they will
become one flesh (Genesis 2:24).*

Do you feel uncomfortable talking with your children about sex? If so, you're not unusual, for many other parents also feel nervous or awkward.

Pray for wisdom and courage to talk with your children. If you don't teach them, you can be sure they will learn about sex from self-exploration, other children, the Internet, TV, school teachers, movies, books, secular music or other sources.

If you don't teach them, your children *will* learn about sex, one way or another. Most of what they learn will be ungodly or inaccurate, and their attitudes are likely to be the same as those of non-Christians,

 *Personal Application*

I need to talk to my children about sexual issues.
❑ Yes ❑ No

Why have you hesitated?

Pray for courage and wisdom to initiate a conversation at the right time.

Teach Values Informally

Teach values through informal family conversations. Make this part of daily living, not just momentous "serious conversations."

The "facts of life" also are important, but godly values are *very* important. Some Scriptures illustrating God's sexual values:

 Therefore God gave them over in the sinful desires of their hearts to sexual impurity for the degrading of their bodies with one another (Romans 1:24).

In the same way the men also abandoned natural relations with women and were inflamed with lust for one another. Men committed inde-

cent acts with other men, and received in themselves the due penalty for their perversion (Romans 1:27).

Do you not know that your bodies are members of Christ himself? Shall I then take the members of Christ and unite them with a prostitute? Never (1 Corinthians 6:16)!

But since there is so much immorality, each man should have his own wife, and each woman her own husband. The husband should fulfill his marital duty to his wife, and likewise the wife to her husband (1 Corinthians 7:2-3).

Flee the evil desires of youth, and pursue righteousness, faith, love and peace, along with those who call on the Lord out of a pure heart (2 Timothy 2:22).

Marriage should be honored by all, and the marriage bed kept pure, for God will judge the adulterer and all the sexually immoral (Hebrews 13:4).

Also read Genesis 1:22, 28; Proverbs 5:15-19; all of the Proverbs; Matthew 5:28 and Matthew 19:3-12.

When you talk, don't simply stress the negatives of sex before marriage. Talk about positive reasons why that is a good policy.

Start talking about values when children are young.

Progressively add more information as they get older. Children vary widely in their maturity levels, so pray for wisdom about when to go into more detail. However, be aware that most parents wait too long and their children begin absorbing information from their culture and their peers at an early age.

Do not encourage premature sexual activity.

My heart breaks when I see young girls wearing makeup and revealing clothes and acting sexy. I'm not suggesting a list of rules, but I am asking you to pay attention—and to pray about what you allow your little girls to wear and how you allow them to act. I'm also suggesting that you evaluate what you give them as presents. Pretty clothes can be fun. But sometimes our gifts encourage wrong attitudes and actions.

Our society puts enough pressure as it is for children to become prematurely sexual. Do what you can to allow your little girls to be little girls, not prematurely sexual children.

Do not overdo "naturalness" about sex.

Some parents overdo "naturalness" because their parents were too grim about sex. Stay balanced. For example, once a child of the opposite sex grows out of infancy, don't shower or bathe together or walk around in the nude.

Teach your children to respect your privacy. Ask them to knock before entering your bedroom.

Build strong relationships with your children.

Sometimes children's sexual activities are the result of not having close relationships with their parents. Make sure your kids don't need to go elsewhere to get love and acceptance.

Demonstrate a good marriage.

Demonstrate affection and respect for your spouse. Likewise, demonstrate respect for those of the opposite sex. If you are a single parent, this can help make up for not being able to demonstrate a good marriage.

If you have marriage problems, or sexual problems, deal with them. Get help.

A related topic: Examine your own example. What TV shows do you watch? What material do you read? Many children learn about sex from their fathers' hidden pornography.

 *Personal Application*

What are some ways you could get an informal talk about sexual topics started?

_____

Have a Formal Talk

The most common error parents make is to wait too long to talk with their children about sex, or not to talk at all. By the time many parents make their first efforts, their children already have been exposed to much ungodly information.

Discuss sex calmly and naturally. Let your children know the subject isn't "dirty." If it would help, visit a Bible bookstore and ask for books that you can study along with your child.

Respond to your children's questions. However, if they do not ask, initiate conversations. If you wait until your children bring up the topic, you may never have the discussion.

On the other hand, beware of information overload—giving too much information at too early an age. Simple information often is all that is needed.

Talk about:

- Your children's coming sexual feelings

- The joy and beauty of a good Christian marriage

- The beauty of sex in marriage

- The simple mechanics of sex

- The sanctity of life and the sin of abortion.

- Not marrying an unbeliever (2 Corinthians 6:14)

- The results of sexual sin

Defuse concerns about homosexuality.

Children sometimes have sexual or romantic thoughts about others of the same sex. It's not unusual for them to engage in same-sex sex play. One of the negative consequences of these fantasies, as well as of the actions, is that children sometimes think this means that they are homosexuals.

If you become aware that your child is struggling with such thoughts, defuse these concerns by saying sexual feelings are normal and that many people have experimented with sex play with others of the same sex. Add that it simply means they were interested in sex, but it certainly doesn't make them a homosexual.

✐ *Personal Application*

If you have not yet talked with your children about sex, when would be a good time? How will you go about starting?

Suggest a "Homework" Assignment

Before your child approaches the age of dating, ask him or her to make two lists.

The first is to list all the qualities or requirements your child expects of the person he or she would want to marry. Suggest that the same standards should apply to dating. Otherwise, if your child dates someone who doesn't meet the criteria, there's a good chance he or she will "fall in love" and abandon the list.

The second list is to list the standards your child will follow when dating in areas such as kissing, hugging and going steady.

Respond Wisely to Sexual Behavior

If you become aware that your child is engaging in some sort of sexual activity, remember to see this as an opportunity for you to help him or her. Do not get hysterical. Do not berate or degrade your child, or say negative things such as, "I know you'll get pregnant by the time you're sixteen."

Make your discussion a mixture of instruction, love and forgiveness, as well as rules and limits.

These guidelines apply to any type of sexual misbehavior, including masturbation, wet dreams, pornography, explicit love letters, sex play or exploration with someone of the same or opposite sex, serious sexual activity and pregnancy.

 *Personal Application*

Write a plan about how you will respond if you become aware that your child has engaged in sexual behavior.

Be Alert for Sexual Abuse

Many children are sexually molested, often without their parents' knowledge. Be alert and take precautions. Train your children to say "no" to inappropriate touching and to tell you if anyone touches them inappropriately. If a child reports something, take it seriously.

It's a hard thing to consider, but incest or molestation sometimes occurs with siblings or other relatives. Many adults with whom I counsel were molested by family members. Train your children in appropriate behavior with family members.

 *Personal Application*

Are you as aware as you need to be about the possibility of sex abuse? ❑ Yes ❑ No

Have you taught your children to say "no" and to tell you about inappropriate touching? ❑ Yes ❑ No

If you answered "no" to the second question, when will you talk with them about this?

Chapter 12

Change Approaches with Teenagers

For the LORD gives wisdom, and from his mouth come knowledge and understanding (Proverbs 2:6).

Many children raised in strong Christian homes go into the world unprepared to live responsibly or to overcome the world's temptations. Sometimes this is because their parents never changed parenting styles and treated sixteen-year-olds the same as they treated three-year-olds.

This is a common mistake. When parents continue to rely on strict rules and "laying down the law" with teenagers, they leave their children woefully unprepared to withstand the temptations they will face in the world after leaving home.

Change your emphasis from training to relationship.

You need God's wisdom in these years, for you are entering a whole new ballgame. Although you trained your children when they were younger, once they hit the teenage years, you will have little success if you continue on that path.

We need to change how we relate to our children as they enter the teenage years. This doesn't mean we abdicate all our authority, but it does mean that we acknowledge that major changes are taking place in our relationship. If we ever need wisdom, it's in knowing how to treat teenagers.

These years are a time of change for children.

These years are a time of change for your children. They are going through the awkward process of developing into the adults they will be apart from you. Among other things, they will be developing their own values, beliefs and relationship with God.

These years are a time of change for you.

These years also can be challenging for you. For example, although you hope your children will become more and more responsible, they may seem to be living in a fog and may seem less responsible than when they were younger. Or they may seem downright rebellious or disrespectful—something you may never have had to deal with before.

Yet you must change your style of parenting to prepare your teenagers for adulthood. What was necessary and appropriate for a three-year old isn't appropriate for a sixteen-year old, even if he or she acts like a three-year old. This often is very difficult for conscientious Christian parents who would like to control every aspect of their children's lives.

You are important to your teenagers.

Since peers become increasingly important to most teenagers, many parents make the mistake of thinking that they are not important to their children. After counseling with hundreds of teenagers, I can assure you this isn't true. Your relationship—the way you treat and communicate with your teenagers—matters a lot to them.

Transfer (Some) Power

Your children will get older and leave home. Your responsibility is to help prepare them for the time they are on their own and making their own decisions.

Some parents stay in the driver's seat right up until the time their children leave home, so the children have not learned how to make decisions or take responsibility. These children often leave home and go wild. (Of course, this isn't the only reason kids go wild. Some simply give in to the flesh and peer pressure.)

Sometimes kids go wild before they leave home. They think they are being treated as children, but they think they are adults. Their reaction is to rebel like children!

A good goal would be to have transferred almost all parental authority by the time children leave home.

Make it a gradual transition.

Parents of infants usually are very directive. That's okay. But starting at a young age, parents should gradually:

- Help their children learn how to make decisions.

- Start giving their children responsibilities.

- Involve their children in joint planning.

- Begin to give their children the authority to make decisions in specified areas.

Choose areas in which you will transfer power.

As your children get older, you and your spouse will need to decide areas in which you are willing to allow your children to make their own decisions—and areas in which you will continue to make decisions. There are no rules about this; each couple will have to define the areas in which they are willing to transfer power.

Reward your children for increasing maturity.

The ideal time to transfer power is when your children act increasingly mature. However, that isn't always possible. If your child seems to be getting less mature, you still should transfer some responsibility even though it has not been "earned." If you don't, you risk sending your child out into the world totally unprepared.

Overview of the rest of this chapter

In the following pages, I will describe some themes that are important in the teenage years. As you read, you will notice that some of them are familiar, for they are continuations of themes that I suggested starting in earlier chapters.

 *Personal Application*

Write a rough schedule of when you think you will transfer power, and at what ages you will make those transfers.

Communicate as Friends

One way to evaluate how you communicate with a teenager is to ask yourself, "Would I talk this way with my next door neighbor?" You still are the parent, but you are in a transition time as your child gets older, and you should be talking with the same respect you use with your neighbor.

You are laying the foundation for a lifetime friendship. Talk as to an older person, not as to a child.

Get to *know* your children.

Get to know your child's heart. Discipline yourself to listen without correcting or admonishing. If you have trouble getting a conversation going, review Chapter 1 for ideas.

Share instead of teaching or lecturing.

Change your teaching style. Shift from an "authoritative" teaching style to a "sharing" style. Lectures are likely to push your child away. If you share from your own experiences, without sounding preachy, your child will be more likely to listen.

One suggestion: Do not say, "I don't want you to go through what I did." This almost always results in the listener rolling his or her eyes and turning you off.

Share your real life experiences and those of others. Don't try to force conversations about "theory" or "doctrine."

Only be careful, and watch yourselves closely so that you do not forget the things your eyes have seen or let them slip from your heart as long as you live. Teach them to your children and to their children after them (Deuteronomy 4:9).

✏ *Personal Application*

Do you need to lecture less and share more?
❏ Yes   ❏ No

How will you remind yourself of this?

Give Emotional Support

Make your home a safe place to be honest, to be accepted, to be loved, to be supported and to be reassured. If your children feel comfortable at home, they may invite their friends to hang out there, and you'll have an even greater opportunity to have an impact on their lives.

One hint: Food is important to teenagers. Visit as you give them snacks. Make warm, friendly family dinners.

Personal Application

Do you need to give more emotional support?
❑ Yes ❑ No

How can you make your home a safe place for your teenagers?

Show a Measure of Forbearance

In some ways, teens remind me of baby giraffes learning how to walk. These are awkward years for your children. There will be stumbles and false starts.

Avoid overreacting to your children's "living in a fog," forgetfulness or irresponsibility. Likewise, give them some breathing room if they seem moody. Show forbearance.

Bear with each other and forgive whatever grievances you may have against one another.

Forgive as the Lord forgave you (Colossians 3:13).

 *Personal Application*

Do you get too irritated with your teenagers? Do you need to give them a little more breathing room?
❑ Yes ❑ No

Write a prayer asking for wisdom, forbearance and patience.

Set Limits as Necessary

Although you are gradually redefining your relationship with your teenagers, always remember you are the parent and be prepared to take action as necessary. Teenagers need to know that there are expectations, rules and consequences. They need the security of knowing that you are in control.

These can be confusing years. Sometimes, your teenagers will need more structure, sometimes less.

Do not let go of everything all at once.

I hope it's obvious by now that I'm not suggesting you let go of all your authority at once. I'm describing a gradual transition process.

Keep track of your children's activities and location.

Ask your children to let you now where they are going and what they will be doing. But, as they grow older and are about ready to leave home, consider phasing this out or relaxing your expectations for up-to-the-minute news.

Be prepared to be *very* authoritative.

If your teenager is acting out seriously, you probably need to be firmer and more controlling. But even when dealing with the most rebellious teenager, look for ways for him or her to earn some power.

Rarely use long-term punishment.

Long-term groundings usually result in more anger and rebellion. We usually used short-term extra chores with our three sons. Groundings were related to specific tasks that had to be accomplished, such as catching up on homework for a class.

✏️ *Personal Application*

Do you maintain the ultimate authority, or have you lost all control? Write any changes you'd like to see, then schedule a family meeting to discuss them.

Realize They'll Be Imperfect at 18

Parents sometimes try to conduct a "crash course" in perfection before their children leave home. This sometimes stems from guilt about their faults as parents or from fear for their children's future.

Yet as children get older, parents are less and less able to force meaningful changes in their behavior or attitudes.

Be prepared for the fact that your children will have unresolved issues when they leave home. Everybody has imperfections, including you and me. Place your children in God's hands, pray for them regularly and trust God.

 Cast all your anxiety on him because he cares for you (1 Peter 5:7).

More Resources

Author, speaker and marriage and family counselor Doug Britton has helped thousands of people since entering the counseling field in 1967. His ministry focuses on showing how to apply the Word of God to daily life in insightful, practical ways.

Online Daily-Living Bible Studies

Visit www.DougBrittonBooks.com to read and print free online Bible studies on marriage, parenting, depression, jealousy, self-concept, temptation, anger and other daily-living topics.

While at the site, sign up to receive one or two emails each month announcing new online studies, as well as news about new books, seminars and retreats with Doug Britton.

Seminars and Retreats

Doug teaches on a wide variety of topics at seminars and retreats. Subject matter includes marriage, parenting, biblical counseling, depression, jealousy and insecurity, self-concept, finances, temptation and anger. For information about sponsoring a seminar or retreat at your church or community center, go to www.DougBrittonBooks.com.

See next page for more resources

Practical Books for Daily Living

Learn how to apply the Bible's truths in all areas of your life. If the following books by Doug Britton are not available at your local bookstore, you can purchase them online at www.DougBrittonBooks.com.

- **Conquering Depression:** A Journey Out of Darkness into God's Light
- **Defeating Temptation:** Biblical Secrets to Self-Control
- **Getting Started:** Taking New Steps in My Walk with Jesus
- **Healing Life's Hurts:** God's Solutions When Others Wound You
- **Overcoming Jealousy and Insecurity:** Biblical Steps to Living without Fear
- **Self-Concept:** Understanding Who You are in Christ
- **Strengthening Your Marriage:** 12 Exercises for Married Couples
- **Successful Christian Parenting:** Nurturing with Insight and Disciplining in Love
- **Victory over Grumpiness, Irritation and Anger**

Marriage by the Book (eight-book series)
- **Book 1 – Laying a Solid Foundation**
- **Book 2 – Making Christ the Cornerstone**
- **Book 3 – Encouraging Your Spouse**
- **Book 4 – Extending Grace to Your Mate**
- **Book 5 – Talking with Respect and Love**
- **Book 6 – Improving Your Teamwork**
- **Book 7 – Putting Money in its Place**
- **Book 8 – Fanning the Flames of Romance**
- **Marriage by the Book Group Leaders' Guide**